D0072619

(Continued)

UNITED WE STAND

*Collaboration
for Child Care and
Early Education Services*

SHARON L. KAGAN

TEACHERS
COLLEGE
PRESS

Teachers College, Columbia University
New York and London

Published by Teachers College Press, 1234 Amsterdam Avenue
New York, NY 10027

Library of Congress Cataloging-in-Publication Data

Kagan, Sharon Lynn.
    United we stand : collaboration for child care and early education services / Sharon L.
Kagan
        p.   cm.—(Early childhood education series)
    Includes bibliographical references and index.
    ISBN 0-8077-3135-8 (alk. paper).
    1. Children—Services for—United States.   2. Child care services—United
States.   3. Early childhood education—United States.
I. Title.   II. Series.
HV741.K27   1991
362.7′0973—dc20   91-26876

Printed on acid-free paper

Manufactured in the United States of America

98 97 96 95 94 93 92 91   8 7 6 5 4 3 2 1

Contents

For the most wonderful instigators and collaborators:

Peter, who felt it should,
Jerry, who knew it could, and
Louis and Ruth, who dreamed it would
Be accomplished.

My love and thanks.

Preface

"There are voices crying what must be done, a hundred, a thousand voices. But what do they help if one seeks for counsel, for one cries this, and one cries that, and another cries something that is neither this nor that."

Alan Paton, *Cry, the Beloved Country*

SUCH AMBIVALENCE OF VOICE has long characterized American child care and early education. Ambling through the decades without strategic vision or sustained commitment, services to young children have been alternatively lauded and condemned, funded and eliminated, debated and debunked. On the one hand, we rhetorically dub children our greatest resource; on the other, they have been accorded low priority in national policy. This volume is a story about why our nation speaks with ambiguous voices about young children and their families, about the consequences of this ambiguity, and about heroic attempts to overcome it. At one level, it is a story about early care and education specifically; at another, it is about American human service delivery generally. At one level, it is a story about the science of collaboration; at another, it is about the artistry of a nation standing united for children and families. It is a tale of irony and optimism.

IN WHAT HAS BEEN CALLED the "greatest analysis of the American way of life" (Jacobson, 1960, p. 148), *Democracy in America*, Alexis de Tocqueville (1838/1947) noted that we Americans share a bemusing passion for creating associations. Whether motivated by democratic ideals to assure involvement of all or by the latent skepticism that elicited our elaborate system of checks and balances, creating associations, organizations, and complex bureaucracies seems to be an inherent characteristic of our national psyche.

And, indeed, where young children and families are concerned, such is the acknowledged case. There is no dearth of organizations, departments, or agencies speaking for youngsters. Precise numbers are enigmatic, but it has been suggested that no less than 31 programs in 11 federal agencies dot the child-care terrain alone (U.S. Department of Labor, 1988). It is not uncommon for states to have scores of agencies dealing with children's issues. Hundreds of professional organizations speak, though rarely in unison, on behalf of children and families. And incoherent policies are proliferated by the staggering numbers of state and federal legislative committees that have jurisdiction for children and families.

On the one hand, such passion for association—noted so many years ago—is cause for celebration. It is the fruition of the twin ideals of democratic participation and effective checks and balances. After all, when optimally functioning, such robust institutional and organizational attention to young children provides untold opportunity for involvement and commitment. On the other hand, scholars and practitioners close to service delivery and policy construction understand that far from ideal, the result is inconsistent, inequitable, insufficient, and ineffective services.

Recognizing the dilemmas, there have been sustained pleas for coordination, consolidation, and collaboration in human services generally, with similar calls resounding through early care and education specifically. For example, bemoaning deep-seated concerns about the inefficiency and insufficiency of America's service to young children and their families, the nation's most prestigious scientific body, the National Academy of Sciences, has issued repeated calls for coordination and collaboration in early care and education. In 1972, it recommended "that a small portion of all federal funds for child care, pre-school educational and related programs . . . be earmarked [to establish] . . . intragovernmental mechanisms for the coordination of the full range of child care and development early education and related health and family service programs" (pp. 41–42). In 1982, the Academy again lamented the lack of coordination in children's services, dubbing it "the . . . unorganized scramble of governmental and nongovernmental representatives for children and families" (p. 76). And again in 1990, the Academy "concludes that planning and coordination must occur at all levels of the policy process . . . [with an] institutional structure that can serve as a focal point for coordinating resources . . . establishing priorities . . . and designing and implementing policy" (p. 310). Such exhortations and demands have not been uncommon. But held hostage to limited budgets and to the primary goals of increasing quantity and quality of services, coordination and collaboration have remained a back-seat issue.

Despite decades of calls that fell on deaf ears, the *Zeitgeist* for collaboration is changing. Pleas for collaboration reverberate through meetings of practitioners, legislative committees, and government agencies. The sentiment is snowballing to such an extent that collaboration has been widely noted in the literature (Gardner, 1990; Gray, 1989; Schorr, 1988) and labeled today's buzzword (Benard, 1989).

Moreover, collaborations are forming in communities and states throughout the nation. Nearly ubiquitous, they know no geographic or disciplinary boundaries. Collaborations are burgeoning in profit, nonprofit, and voluntary sectors in our country and abroad in fields as diverse as education, health, psychology, mental health, business, industry, and the arts. Whether they are termed partnerships, linkages, cooperatives, or roundtables, their very existence acknowledges that America is at the brink of a practical renaissance, reshaping how it wants to deliver goods and services.

Such enthusiasm for collaboration has not escaped human services, where collaborations are being regarded as essential catalysts for system reform. Fueled by desires to improve the quality and distribution of services, the need for services to be maximally cost-effective and family-responsive, and the recognition that the complex needs of today's families often transcend rigid bureaucratic and policy structures, collaborations are being formed with the broad goal of improving services to children and families (Levy & Copple, 1989).

Recalling past efforts and endemic challenges, today's call for collaboration is also resounding loudly in child care and early education. While emanating from a long history of inequitable policies, dysfunctional practices, and disproportionate shares of financial and public support, interest in collaboration in early care and education has increased dramatically. In large part, this is due to new interest in the field. Accelerated by rapidly changing demographics and data affirming the benefits of early intervention to low-income children, America has awakened to the importance of early intervention. Such realizations have been supported and advanced by new constituents including businesspeople and politicians from both sides of the aisle who are now acknowledging what the field has long understood—that the care young children receive is inseparable from their learning, and learning is inseparable from care.

Further, solid links between care and education are evident within the field. At the service level, parents and providers are joining forces, and agencies that render different services are forming councils and task forces to address common issues. At the policy level, a renewed emphasis on fostering private- and public-sector partnerships and on stimulating more effective public-sector service delivery has led to the inclusion of collaborative provisions in countless reports (Committee for Economic Development, 1987; Council of Chief State

School Officers, 1989; National Conference of State Legislatures, 1989; National Governors' Association, 1987) and in state and federal legislation, including the 1988 Family Support Act and the 1986 amendments to the Education for All Handicapped Children Act (P.L. 99-457).

Despite this historic and current recognition of the need for collaboration and its growing popularity, opinions about collaboration vary widely. Some view collaboration as the natural response to a changing *Zeitgeist*, an obvious strategy to address the inadequacies of an increasingly bureaucratic and technologically sophisticated social order. Others see it as a potential panacea, an inventive and long-absent strategy that provides the promise of addressing, at worst, and solving, at best, intractable social service delivery problems. In the middle are the skeptical optimists, who hope that collaboration will fulfill its potential but recognize the persistent challenges it presents.

Ambiguity surrounding the outcome of collaboration is matched by ambiguity surrounding its process, rationale, and history in early care and education. Though unfortunate, such confusion is fueled by the lack of (1) a systematic investigation of the evolution of collaboration as a social construct as it relates to the field, (2) an analysis of the evolution of collaboration within the field itself, and (3) a distillation of the many frameworks developed for understanding collaboration that may be germane to early care and education. The absence of such codified knowledge is particularly unfortunate because robust information on the topic exists in educational, psychosocial, economic, and political literatures.

This volume on collaboration in child care and early education attempts to fill that void. It is premised on the belief that there is much to learn about collaboration from other disciplines and the private sector and that such knowledge, when applied, can help improve services to young children and their families. Yet because the related material is so voluminous, the reader should note that this volume is, of necessity, selective rather than comprehensive. It is an attempt to extract from the literature and practice those events, issues, and constructs most relevant to enhancing understanding of collaboration's evolution, rationale, and practice in early care and education.

With that goal in mind, the volume is divided into ten chapters. The first, "A Preamble: Defining Collaboration," offers an analysis of the debate over the definitions of collaboration and postulates the definition used throughout the document. The second, "The Social Context for Collaboration," traces the evolution of collaboration as a construct outside the field of early care and education, drawing heavily on literature from economics, business, and organizational psychology. Chapter 3, "Valuing Collaboration: Its Rationale and Benefits," presents the rationale of and benefits for collaboration as discussed in the general literature. Chapter 4, "Understanding the Collaborative Process," distills numerous frameworks that have been advanced to understand collaborative functioning. The chapter offers a conceptual framework that combines many of these and is particularly sensitive to the challenges faced by practitioners in the field of early care and education.

Having established the definition, context, rationale, and process of collaboration, the discussion turns to the implementation of collaboration in early care and education. The fifth chapter, "The Odyssey of Collaboration in Early Care and Education," traces the evolution of the need for collaboration in the field. Drawing on sources from history, psychology, education, and human service literatures, this chapter elucidates the historic events that yielded today's income-segregated, fragmented, and inequitable service delivery system. Chapter 6, "Rectifying the Problems: Calls to Collaborate," recounts the often troublesome journey to the present, highlighting episodic collaborative attempts, particularly those of the past two decades, that have sought to overcome prevailing systemic inadequacies. The seventh chapter, "The Special Case of Special Education," discusses the accelerative role of special education legislation in fostering collaboration in the field.

The final three chapters address the current state of collaboration in early care and education. Chapter 8, "The Labyrinth of Current Collaborative Efforts," discusses the current collaborative context and provides a panorama of current early care and education collaborations. Chapter 9, "Sacred Cows and Sacrificial Lambs: Lessons from Recent Collaborations," extracts lessons for present-day practice from work being undertaken in the field. Chapter 10, "United We Stand: Facing Future Issues," discusses the challenges that those interested in collaboration will need to address if collaboration is to reach its full potential. The volume concludes with an Appendix of program descriptions of early care and education collaborations at work.

Many people contributed to the development of this volume. Particular thanks are extended to Darlene DeRose, whose knowledge of the private sector and tenacity in researching and drafting several chapters extended my knowledge and vision. Deborah Lonow and Jessica Levin were helpful in refining the conceptual model offered in the fourth chapter. Gwen Morgan and Tutti Sherlock lent wisdom and materials regarding the evolution of America's resource and referral movement. Ann Rivera and Faith Lamb-Parker, valued collaborators, lent insight and support in the study that advanced much of the thinking in Chapters 9 and 10. Susan Schultheiss rendered most helpful editorial assistance. Finally, I am deeply indebted to the collaborators—many whose work is chronicled in the Appendix—who allowed me a brief glimpse of their magnificent visions.

I would like to thank the Smith Richardson Foundation for their support of the Bush Center at Yale and Edward Zigler for his support of my work. Very special thanks are extended to Vivien Stewart, Michael Levine, and Sheila Smith (formerly) of the Carnegie Corporation of New York, as well as Marilyn Segal and Luba Lynch and the A. L. Mailman Family Foundation for financial and spiritual support. Their commitment to collaboration as a concept and to me as an individual has made this work possible.

UNITED WE STAND

*Collaboration
for Child Care and
Early Education Services*

CHAPTER 1

A Preamble:
Defining Collaboration

GIVEN THAT GREAT AMBIGUITY surrounds the definition of *collaboration*, it is necessary to begin the discussion by ferreting out what the literature offers as meanings of the term and identifying the definition that will be used throughout this volume. Unfortunately, this is not a simple task. Of all the misuses of the construct *collaboration*, three categories appear to be most typical: first, those that confuse collaboration with strategies used to achieve it; second, those that confuse collaboration with other entities; and third, those that confuse collaboration with its kindred processes—coordination and cooperation.

In the first category—collaboration as operational strategies—collaboration is often equated with "linkages." In this document, as in much of the literature, linkages and collaboration are distinguished from one another, with linkages referring to mechanisms established among agencies in order to make the collaboration work (Flynn & Harbin, 1987; Galaskiewicz & Shatin, 1981; Skaff, 1988; Stafford, Rog, & Vander Meer, 1984; Tindall et al., 1982).

In the second category, collaboration is used interchangeably with other entities—consortia, collectives, and even interorganizational relationships. Adhering to this perspective, Intriligator (1986) claims that collaborative arrangements can be called interorganizational relationships, consortia, collaboratives, or collectives. Goldring (1986) explains that collaborations have entered the common parlance under the name consortium. For purposes of this volume, we shall use *collaboration* as the generic term encompassing a variety of entities including councils, task forces, consortia, interagency cabinets, coalitions, and committees. Herein, interorganizational relations will be regarded as a discipline that emerged from the study of organizational behavior and larger social units (Gamm, 1981).

However troublesome these categories, the third category—that which very often equates *collaboration* with its allied terms *cooperation* and *coordination*—is the most problematic and the subject of most debate in the literature. Part of the difficulty arises because the synonymous use of the three terms—cooperation, coordination and collaboration—is sanctioned. The American Psychological Association (1988) and the U.S. Department of Education (1986) classify collaboration as a synonym "used for" cooperation. The problem is further exacerbated because different scholars imbue the terms with their own unique meanings. Distinguishing the terms according to their spheres of influence, Elder and Magrab (1980), for example, define *coordination* as cooperative efforts within an agency and *collaboration* as coordinated efforts across agencies.

Despite confusion and individual interpretation, a common view, which this analysis supports, is emerging in the literature. It suggests that cooperation, coordination, and collaboration are quite different and constitute a hierarchy or ladder (Black & Kase, 1963; Elder & Magrab, 1980; Hord, 1986; Morgan, 1985; Schwartz, 1981; Stafford et al., 1984). As one progresses from cooperation through coordination to collaboration, interorganizational relationships become more sophisticated, complex, and effective for problem solving.

Among those who accept the hierarchical definitions, there is little disagreement that cooperation forms the base; it is the least formal and the most prevalent. Grounded in personal relationships, cooperation exists without any clearly defined structure. At the cooperative level, organizations work informally together. Often, they have only a superficial awareness of one another's full array of programs and goals. In fact, cooperation can occur despite differing goals (Lanier, 1980; Derlega & Grzelak, 1982). Participants and organizations that cooperate retain their independent full autonomy, so that power is neither shared among them nor yielded to a third party (Hord, 1986). Moreover, it is important to note that, in a cooperation, resources are not necessarily pooled (Hord, 1986).

As one progresses up the hierarchy to coordination and collaboration, there is slightly less definitional agreement. Some authors claim that both coordination and collaboration are vague and ill-defined (Flynn & Harbin, 1987; Weiss, 1981). Others suggest that there is little real distinction between the these two "higher-level" terms (Hord, 1980, 1985; Houston, 1979; Kraus, 1980). Those who see little difference between coordination and collaboration typically regard them as relational systems that consist of two or more participants (Appley & Winder, 1977a; Gray, 1985; Intriligator, 1986; Johnson, McLaughlin, & Christensen, 1982).

Practical and theoretical reasons exist for equating coordination and collaboration. On the practical side, many documented coordination efforts began in the 1960s, just about the time collaboration was being advanced as an ideal. Because collaboration was a new and unfamiliar concept, *coordination* was the term applied to the reality of practice and thus dominated the dialogue. Over time, coordination and collaboration came to be used synonymously in everyday discourse. On the theoretical side, many scholars feel little difference exists between coordination and collaboration because they share important characteristics: mutuality of goals, resource sharing or pooling among group members, and dynamic, changing interactions (Stafford et al., 1984).

Despite these rationales, a growing body of literature separates the two higher levels of the hierarchy. Coordination is now more commonly regarded as a prerequisite for collaboration (Hord, 1986) and is conceptualized as a less complex and sophisticated construct than collaboration. Certainly, coordination entails efforts to smooth relationships among organizations and often results in specific modifications in the way agencies operate. But in coordinated efforts, agencies remain independent (Morris & Lescohier, 1978). In contrast, collaboration brings previously separated organizations into a new structure (Morris & Lescohier, 1978). Melaville and Blank (1991) posit that the advantage of collaboration is that it affords the opportunity to restructure the expertise and resources of partner agencies. Aside from restructuring, recent literature suggests that other important characteristics distinguish coordination and collaboration. Collaboration implies a greater sharing of resources, more intense joint planning, and the sharing of power and authority. Kraus (1980) affirms the point by noting that collaboration is a "cooperative venture based on shared power and authority." Though appearing subtle, the differences are important because egalitarian power relationships entail processes and produce consequences quite unlike those where power and resources are not distributed. Such practical differences further explain why distinguishing collaboration from coordination and placing it at the apex of the cooperation-coordination-collaboration troika is gaining currency.

Accepting this increasingly supported approach, this analysis regards collaboration as a construct that is different from, and more complex than, coordination or cooperation. Herein, collaborations are defined as organizational and interorganizational structures where resources, power, and authority are shared and where people are brought together to achieve common goals that could not be accomplished by a single individual or organization independently.

CHAPTER 2

The Social Context for Collaboration

[Collaboration] "is as fundamental to the successful building of a post-industrial order as competition was to the successful building of an industrial order."

Eric Trist, 1977

NOTING THE INADEQUACIES of the prevailing bureaucratic system, major thinkers more than 25 years ago began to envision and write about a new social system for the future. They predicted that organizational survival in the postindustrial world would depend less on competition and more on the recognition and realization of organizational interdependence. Propelling the scholarly ethos of the time, Bennis (1966) wrote, "I see democracy, collaboration and science as three broad streams moving toward confluence in the twentieth century" (p. 2). Underscoring the new importance he accorded collaboration, Bennis believed that multiple organizational and value changes, demographic shifts, and dissatisfaction with the existing human services delivery system would be natural catalysts for greater collaboration. Bennis's beliefs, confirmed by others, seem to have been accurate. As the following sections indicate, the call for collaboration is rooted in an organizational paradigm shift, in changing values, perceptions, and demographics, and in a growing dissatisfaction with America's delivery system for human services.

THE ORGANIZATIONAL PARADIGM SHIFT

Organizations in today's postindustrial society face a markedly different environment from those of their predecessors in the preindustrial and industrial periods. Characterized by a slow rate of change, the preindustrial and industrial organizational orders were comparatively stable (Appley & Winder, 1977b; Bennis, 1966). Such stability supported a hierarchical structure of bureaucracy and enabled managers to focus attention primarily on the internal workings of the organization. This ethos fostered organizational independence wherein each organization acted separately from others, earning them the title of "closed" systems (Gamm, 1983). Buoyed by a value system based on Darwin's theory of the survival of the fittest, by principles of the free market, and by beliefs that human, fiscal, and physical resources were in short supply, organizations engaged in fierce competitive behavior among themselves. Thus, despite societal stability, organizations were competitive and there were no incentives or perceived needs for collaboration.

In contrast, postindustrial society is marked by turbulence, complexity, and uncertainty (Appley & Winder, 1977b; Bennis, 1966; Emery & Trist, 1973; Trist, 1977). Advancements in science and technology have made work more technical and management more complicated. The economy has become a roller coaster, with recessions followed by hyperinflation, high interest rates, and deeper recessions. Compounding this upheaval, in the 1970s and 1980s major energy crises, labor shortages, new environmental policies, deregulation, and a dramatic rise in foreign competition demanded a new approach to business. The previously functional closed system became dysfunctional, giving way to a more open system (Gamm, 1983). To be effective, managers recognized that they needed to anticipate and deal with both external and internal forces; preserving the status quo and simply managing risk would not suffice.

As organizations struggled to craft missions and strategies responsive to increased technological sophistication and specialization, a new management perspective evolved. Managers realized that organizational survival was predicated on their ability to develop and convert strategic plans to operational plans. To do so, organizations needed to think inclusively and to convert their "command" organizations to "team" organizations, soliciting collaborative input from all workers. Japanese success, attributed in part to effective teamwork, did not escape the attention of corporate America. New intraorganizational and interorganizational perspectives helped to realign relationships within and between organizations.

WORKERS' CHANGING VALUES

In addition to confronting massive pressures related to productivity and the demands of an increasingly complex and uncertain world, organizations have faced internal pressures resulting from the changing value systems of American workers. Without question, the civil rights movement left a legacy that transcended issues of minorities' rights. In raising American consciousness about fairness and equity, the civil rights movement not only helped empower the disenfranchised but also fostered the desire for self-worth, involvement, and validation among women, the handicapped, and workers. Interestingly, and not coincidentally, the new values being expressed—individual fulfillment, autonomy, cooperation, participation in workplace decisions (Carew, 1976; Kanter, 1983; Kraus, 1980; Slater, 1970; Trist, 1976)—were not inconsistent with collaborative relationships and structures being called for in organizations. Another factor responsible for such changes in worker values was an unprecedented increase in the educational level of workers (Kanter, 1983). With increased education came the confidence and technical expertise that created a demand for a more interactive and less supervisorial management style. The new workforce demanded a reorientation in structure that led to more collaborative and integrative work processes.

These changes in worker values are important because they impact organizations directly. The literature notes that ideas and values of organizations derive in part from those of its employees (Brewer & deLeon, 1983; Greenfield, 1973) and that successful organizations are those in which the corporate value system is compatible with employees' personal value systems (Kraus, 1980). Consequently, motivated by the knowledge that workers wanted to be more involved and by the researched benefits of such involvement, particularly as evidenced in Japan, corporate America turned to collaboration, at least in principle.

THE IMPACT OF THE ECOLOGICAL PERSPECTIVE

Practical motivations in the form of organizational effectiveness were not the sole rationale for a new commitment to collaboration. Simultaneously, theoretical work—including new ideas about the interrelatedness of the individual, family, and community—also helped shape the ethos of collaboration. Often referred to as the ecological perspective advanced by Urie Bronfenbrenner (1979), this vision recognized that individuals are part of a broad network that they impact and that dramatically impacts them. As this ecological and holistic orientation took hold, many practical consequences emerged. Long-discrete entities—including the worlds of home and work, and for children, home and schools—have become intertwined. At a personal level, young professionals came to realize the strategic importance of linking with one another and with older adults as they sought career opportunities. Networking became an accepted and necessary activity. For individuals and businesses, the concept of independence was replaced by a focus on interdependence.

For those in the human services, the ecological orientation took on special meaning. For some, it became the scapegoat for the intractability of social problems, the rationale for a quagmired system. After all, it certainly was easier to treat one aspect of a problem rather than the whole, to address the problems of an individual as opposed to overwhelming societal problems. For other social scientists and human service providers, the ecological orientation brought with it an alternate framework—a systems perspective—for addressing service delivery problems. Understanding that fragmentation, duplication of services, and inequity are the undesirable but inevitable results of the current delivery system, policy makers called for a systems approach, an integrated strategy that would address the need for collaboration among systems and disciplines.

THE IMPACT OF CHANGING DEMOGRAPHICS

Early in the twentieth century, the American family evidenced comparative stability in relationships, occupations, and even geographic locale. But as technology became more sophisticated and urbanization increased, and as the impact of societal changes became manifest, stable America became more transient. As a result of the women's movement, many women—traditionally the keepers of home and family—sought greater economic independence. Of greater significance, recessions and underemployment reduced the ability of families to survive on only one income. The median annual earnings of the head of a family under age 30 with children declined by 39 percent between 1973 and 1986. Despite efforts of women to compensate for the reduced earnings of spouses by joining the workforce in unprecedented numbers, real family income has remained below the 1973 levels for over a decade (Rosewater, 1989). Increased divorce rates, escalating numbers of single-parent families, and the feminization of poverty characterize the new demographics. Increased family stress is manifest in growing annual percentages of child and spouse abuse (National Committee for the Prevention of Child Abuse, 1988; U.S. Bureau of Justice Statistics, 1986) and in increases in alcoholism and drug abuse (National Institute on Drug Abuse, 1987). Poverty has taken on dimensions and proportions never before seen (Ellwood, 1988; Wilson, 1987).

As the magnitude of social problems escalated, so did their complexity. Once more narrowly isolated, social problems now began to cut across the human condition. Health problems could not be isolated from social service needs; educational problems were meshed with welfare issues. Human need was not neatly categorized by bureaucratic agency; it transcended organizational structures. Consequently, virtually every social institution was affected by the press for more services and more effective services. Unable to expand at a pace commensurate with the burgeoning social problems, health, welfare, and education systems were accused of mismanagement and inefficient and insufficient services. A sense of crisis permeated the human service delivery system (Gage, 1976), accompanied by a barrage of specific accusations of fragmentation, duplication of services, and wasted resources (Gamm, 1983). In spite of growing need, there were no incentives for collaboration; in fact, agency insularity was rewarded.

As public need increased and as institutional problems became more numerous and complex, human service agencies faced soaring costs to meet the challenges at hand. But reconciling increased costs with decreased performance was a bitter pill an increasingly conservative public would not swallow. Bureaucratic requests for additional funds often fell on the deaf ears of disenchanted and fiscally constrained policy makers.

Faced with a crisis of confidence, critical human and technological resource shortages, and escalating public demands, human service agencies began to think more creatively and turned to collaboration as one means of coping with the tremendous challenges they faced. For example, schools actively began to collaborate with business and industry, so that by 1986, more than 40,000 school-business partnerships existed in the nation (Otterbourg & Timpane, 1986). Health and education institutions formed health/education collaboratives. In nearly every corner of the human service sector, recognition of the limitations of the extant human services delivery structure and its legacy of inadequate services propelled collaboration forward.

CHAPTER 3

Valuing Collaboration:
Its Rationale and Benefits

[The value of a collaboration is its] "affirmation of our hopes for change, rationality, efficiency and comprehensiveness."

Janet Weiss, 1981

GIVEN THIS HISTORY, it is not surprising that theorists and service providers have turned to collaboration as a means of meeting the changing service needs of a demanding public. Often, the benefits expected from collaboration constitute its rationale. Organizations are motivated to participate in collaborations not because they offer heuristic appeal but because they offer the potential of alleviating organizational ills while hastening concrete gains. Theorists and practitioners suggest that the rationale for and benefits of collaboration fall into four major categories: (1) alleviating scarcity of resources, (2) expanding the narrowness of problem conceptualization, (3) improving inadequacies in human service delivery, and (4) achieving organizational reform.

ALLEVIATING SCARCITY OF RESOURCES

One of the most frequently mentioned rationales for and benefits of collaboration is overcoming a scarcity of resources (Appley & Winder, 1977a; Kraus, 1980; Schermerhorn, 1975; Schindler-Rainman, 1981). Broadly defined by theorists, resources are categorized as fiscal, physical, and human. Agencies face resource limitations in each category: budget cuts dominate program operations; facilities are aging; and the pool of qualified employment candidates continues to shrink. In an effort to minimize the threat to organizational efficacy, agencies collaborate, hoping to increase access to or compensate for badly needed resources. Given the recent moves toward public accountability on the part of government agencies, the resources rationale gains even greater currency.

The literature suggests that it is not unreasonable to expect enhanced resource utilization as a result of collaborative efforts. Collaborations claim to minimize administrative expenses and improve administrative efficiency (Burgard, 1983; Weiss, 1981). They capitalize on the largest number of resources at the smallest cost, sometimes uncovering unused resources (Burgard, 1983; Johnson et al., 1982; Lippitt & Van Til, 1981). Resources are used better and are wasted less, particularly with respect to resource overlaps (Gamm, 1983; Jones 1975; Loadman, Parnick, & Schober, 1981; O'Connor, Albrecht, Cohen, & Newquist-Carroll, 1984; Rogers & Mulford, 1982; Schaffer & Bryant, 1983; Schindler-Rainman, 1981; Trist, 1977; Urban and Rural Systems Associates, 1977; Weiss, 1981). The division of labor, sharing of facilities, and pooling of information are believed to improve use of the scarce resources allocated to participants.

Though the majority of authors see scarcity of resources as a major rationale for and benefit of collaboration, some disagree. They argue instead that competition, not collaboration, is based on the assumption that resources are scarce (Appley & Winder, 1977a; Kraus, 1980). In fact, organizations might be discouraged from collaborating if they believe their already scarce resources will be depleted by sharing with competitors (Molnar, 1978). The achievement of true collaboration, they argue, requires a belief in "nonscarcity structure," in which resources in general are believed to be abundant, although specific resources may be limited (Appley & Winder, 1977a; Kraus, 1980).

EXPANDING PROBLEM CONCEPTUALIZATION

A second rationale for and benefit of collaboration, much mentioned in the literature, relates to how organizations can overcome their tendency to view problems from individual (and sometimes narrow) perspectives. For example, Gray (1985) claims that an organization's inability to adapt to a new environment lies in its failure to conceptualize a problem and analyze potential solutions at a level where the organization is joined by other similarly concerned individuals, groups, and/or organizations. This level of interaction, born of mutual interests or concerns, is known as the "domain level."

A domain can be thought of as the organization's field of activity or niche in the market and includes the organization's purpose, clients, products, and/or income sources. Domains typically fall into three categories: similar, symbiotic, or different. Gamm (1983) and Trist (1983) suggest that the domain category affects how and if collaborative relationships develop. For example, if domain similarity exists, two or more agencies share purposes, clients, products, or income sources. Such similarity may lead either to collaboration or to competition among the agencies (Gamm, 1983). If agencies fall into the symbiotic category, typically one organization offers important services to another through a network or central organization (Trist, 1983). Such a pattern often implies a hierarchical, rather than egalitarian, relationship. Finally, different domains, where none of the elements is shared, also predict hierarchical relationships wherein one organization looks to the other as a "standard-setter" (Gamm, 1983).

The domain construct is helpful on several counts. First, it acknowledges that the nature of collaboration is somewhat predictable, based on the alignment of critical variables. Second, Gray (1985) points out that organizations can use this construct as they encounter practical challenges such as coping with resource scarcity. And third, the domain construct is useful as agencies broaden their conceptualizations of the problems and their potential solutions, particularly with regard to agency interdependencies.

CORRECTING INADEQUACIES IN SERVICE DELIVERY

A third rationale for collaboration rests on dissatisfaction with and a related desire to improve direct services and the service delivery system.

With respect to improving direct services, the literature indicates that this is not an unrealistic expectation. Collaborative activity is believed to "enrich services" (O'Connell, 1985) and to render them more comprehensive, accessible, and creative (Gamm, 1983; Hord, 1980; Johnson et al., 1982; Kagan, 1989; Levy & Copple, 1989; Lippitt & Van Til, 1981; Olsen, 1983; Schindler-Rainman, 1981; Stafford et al., 1984; Weiss, 1981; Zeller, 1980).

Beyond improvement in service delivery, collaborations are judged by some to be a vital solution to the inadequacies and inflexibilities of bureaucracy (Bennis, 1966; Kraus, 1980; Levy & Merry, 1986; McNulty, 1983). Severe systemic inadequacies—including inflexibility in the face of change and uncertainty, ineffective communication systems caused by hierarchical divisions, and unequal power distribution—have prompted theorists to argue that we must replace bureaucracy with more collaborative forms of organization.

Recognizing the challenges facing bureaucracies in the public and private sector, some important reform efforts of the 1960s and 1970s advocated collaboration and services integration. Such efforts aimed to achieve the coordinated delivery of services. For example, the proposed Allied Services Act of 1972, later reintroduced in 1974, would have "enabled states with approved plans to transfer up to 30% of federal categorical funds from certain designated programs to related human services programs included in their plan" (Gage, 1976, p. 29). And indeed, the passage of the Education for All Handicapped Children Act of 1975 mandated coordination among service providers. Prior to the law, coordinated planning was voluntary, after the "more essential business was completed" (Martinson, 1982, p. 390). Head Start mandated important collaborations with parents, as did Elementary and Secondary Education Act (ESEA) Title I (now Chapter 1). With these mandates, the need for systematic reform and the use of collaboration to achieve it was legislatively validated.

Manifestations of private-sector collaboration differ slightly from those in the nonprofit sector. For-profit organizations, pressed by shareholder and market demands, turned to global interdependencies in the form of the multinational corporation, a structure termed the new organizational form (Hancock, 1983). Internally, these corporations have attempted to alter organizational culture by fostering open communication, teamwork, and interdependence among work groups and by replacing hierarchical authority with task forces and self-managed teams.

ACHIEVING ORGANIZATIONAL REFORM

Some who are more skeptical of the direct service and systemic contributions of collaboration suggest that it may at least have social or organizational benefits. Warren (1973) argues that to understand the current trend toward collaboration, in the absence of empirical results, one must look to its latent functions. These are the "objective consequences of a social practice or belief contributing to the adjustment or adaptation of a system which are neither intended nor recognized" (p. 360). Collaborations reduce the threat of competition, ensure that agencies will have a say in decisions, and promote agency viability and expansion. Warren claims that collaboration "gives the aura of change without affecting either the causes or the basic injustices in the social system" (1973, p. 361). Weiss (1981) agrees. Pointing to the "indifferent success, the costs, and the conflict surrounding real-world collaborations" (p. 40), Weiss suggests that collaborations serve a symbolic rather than substantive function. Recognizing that our human services system is inadequate, decision makers turn to collaboration as evidence of their efforts to structure and simplify the system, instead of reforming the system itself. The intangible success of coordination reform, as Weiss (1981) calls it, lies in its ability to evoke certain shared social values.

Less skeptical than Warren and Weiss, other theorists suggest that collaboration is more than symbolic, that it plays a very real role in increasing communication, enhancing collective problem solving, and boosting worker productivity. Not only will communication be improved and increased via collaboration (Kraus, 1980; Lippitt & Van Til, 1981; O'Connell, 1985; Weiss, 1981), but its benefits will extend to other activities. Planning is better when individuals and organizations work together (Lippitt & Van Til, 1981). With improved communication, personnel exhibit increased morale and productivity because they are informed about and involved in organizational efforts (Kraus, 1980; Schindler-Rainman, 1981). Increased communication may enable the group to function as a more unified whole, and in so doing the group may have more influence on its external environment (Schindler-Rainman, 1981).

The collaborative process gives evidence of creating energy among participants that results in better problem-solving behavior. Risk taking is increased, which brings with it new ideas and more creativity. Morale is boosted, and productivity and motivation are increased (Fox & Faver, 1984; Kraus, 1980; Schindler-Rainman, 1981). Such boosts in worker productivity and innovative programs may yield increased commitment on the part of employees and users (Burgard, 1983; Goldring, 1986; Weiss, 1981). Not insignificant accomplishments in their own right, these outcomes are also important prerequisites for improved service delivery (Levy & Copple, 1989).

Collaboration, then, is valued for the inadequacies and inconsistencies it hopes to overcome. The anticipated benefits—alleviating scarce resources, expanding problem conceptualization, improving service delivery, and achieving organizational reform—constitute the rationale for the existence of collaborative entities.

Given this understanding of *why* collaborations exist, we turn to a discussion of *how* they function.

CHAPTER 4

Understanding the Collaborative Process

"[The concept] is difficult to define and understand. Its broad, complex, multidimensional, interactional, developmental nature makes implementation difficult."

Harbin and McNulty, 1990

THE LITERATURE IS REPLETE with information about the collaborative process, with some of the most lucid and insightful commentary emanating from practitioners. By coupling their firsthand knowledge with that of academics, many of whom have studied collaboration for decades and/or evaluated or implemented collaborations, the synopsis below provides a theoretical framework for understanding a very practical process.

A review of the literature indicates that collaborations have much in common structurally. All collaborations seem to pass through common developmental stages. Highly predictable, these stages follow in sequence. But the pace and the trajectory through which the stages are achieved are idiosyncratic to particular collaborations. This suggests that certain mediating variables (goals, resources, power and authority, and levels of adaptiveness) alter the pace of implementation to yield individually distinct collaborative processes. Like stages, the categories of variables are also quite universal. Less predictable than the stages, however, mediating variables differ in intensity and in their impact on the collaborative process. The framework below, culled from many sources, suggests that it is a combination of the normal development stages and the individual mediating variables that influences the pace and outcome of the collaboration. (Occurring in much the same way, normal human development is the product of the intersection of universal developmental stages and individual mediating variables, for example, intelligence, temperament, and socioeconomic status. Together, they mesh in highly idiosyncratic ways, yielding an infinite variety of personalities.)

14

DEVELOPMENTAL STAGES

The organizational development literature is replete with theories that discuss the stages of organizational development and provide the basis from which theories about collaborative development have emerged. Lewin (1951), an early stage theorist, suggested that the process of organizational change can be described in three stages: unfreezing, moving, and refreezing. Picturesque and revealing, these words suggest both the static (frozen) nature of organizations and the "hoped-for" dynamic (moving). Lewin's stages have been reinterpreted and embellished in the decades since their introduction. Reitz (1987) and Cummings and Huse (1989), for example, have suggested that these periods reflect the natural stages wherein the need for change is recognized, acted on, and institutionalized. Others suggest four stages. Levy (1986) identifies decline, transformation, transition, and stabilization/development. Hage and Aiken (1970) label them evaluation, initiation, implementation, and routinization.

In discussing the stages of collaborative process, although authors use different nomenclature, they tend to agree on the sequence and basic activities within each stage. The stages of collaborative evolution have been alternatively termed aspects of domain formation (Trist, 1983), sequential phases (McCann, 1983), and steps in the process of interagency collaboration (Lippitt & Van Til, 1981). Four stages suggested by Flynn and Harbin (1987)—formation, conceptualization, development, and implementation—combined with two stages—evaluation and termination—from Brewer and deLeon (1983) convey the range of stages described in the literature. It should be noted that progression through the stages is typically linear, but a change in mission or direction, or a reassessment of the collaborative structure, may necessitate a transition back to a previous stage (Flynn & Harbin, 1987). Further, although these stages appear fairly neat and orderly on paper, in reality they overlap.

Formation

During the formation stage, a number of important activities take place that will shape all future stages. First, the idea for the collaboration is born: Lippitt and Van Til (1981) call this articulation of the vision. The vision arises in response to recognition or identification of a potential or real problem. Formation is underway when an individual conceptualizes an effort or strategy to resolve the problem.

Once a conceptual initiator emerges, the problem and the vision must be shared. During the formation stage, group members are identified and recruited, often by the initiating individual or organization. Gray (1985) calls this process identification of stakeholders. The initiator presents the rationale for the collaboration to the stakeholders, so that they begin to recognize and appreciate their interdependence (Gray, 1985; Lippitt & Van Til, 1981).

Following the identification of the group members, the collaboration explores the viability of the vision. Lippitt and Van Til (1981) refer to this activity as "testing the collaborative waters" (p. 8). Members become acquainted with one another and their programs, in part to find out if the collaboration will threaten organizational turf (Lippitt & Van Til, 1981). At this point, a global mission will be identified and discussed (Flynn & Harbin, 1987; Lippitt & Van Til, 1981).

Conceptualization

The conceptualization phase is reached when the collaboration's participants adopt a formal policy statement and objectives. This phase is also referred to as direction setting (McCann, 1983; Trist, 1983). Individual expectations about the future of the collaboration and the activating forces behind each member's participation are shared. Participants identify a common purpose, develop a common interpretation of the future, and agree on a path to achieve it (Gray, 1985; Trist, 1983).

Because this phase requires active member commitment and participation, tasks, roles, and responsibilities are discussed during conceptualization. Theorists agree that clear definitions of member and team roles must be developed at this point (Flynn & Harbin, 1987; Lippitt & Van Til, 1981; O'Connell, 1985). Such role assignment enables the group to select a decision-making model and to develop an administrative structure for future interagency activities (Flynn & Harbin, 1987).

Development

The third stage involves the development of a formal structure that will sustain the conceptualization and the collaboration. The development stage has alternately been termed "putting the meat on the bones" (Flynn & Harbin, 1987, p. 40) and "institutionalizing the shared meanings and prevailing norms" of the collaboration (Gray, 1985, p. 913). The vision and the formal mission are now transformed from philosophy to practice.

During the development stage, the group creates permanent

structures and begins the productive work of identifying programs for revision or expansion. The structures are internal and facilitate participant accommodation of partially conflicting interests (Trist, 1983). Structures include work-group assignments, establishment of a communication system (Flynn & Harbin, 1987), and selection of locales (Trist, 1983). The productive work includes addressing and resolving issues and conflicts within the group, developing plans, and obtaining approval of key decision makers (Flynn & Harbin, 1987).

Implementation

If the group has successfully passed through the first three stages, the collaboration is ready to implement its programs. This stage can be called action-intervention, since the proposed revisions are put into practice (Margulies & Raia, 1972). Decisions made during the earlier stages are now carried out at the administrative and service delivery levels. Necessary policy changes are made, agencies interact according to the agreed-upon structures, and services ideally are improved (Flynn & Harbin, 1987).

Evaluation

Evaluation is an essential and continuous phase of collaboration. It is a process whereby actual performance levels are compared to expectations (Brewer & deLeon, 1983). Lippitt and Van Til (1981) describe this stage as "renewal and review of the validity of the dream that brought the collaboration into existence" (p. 10). In this stage, participants seek to discover if they have been successful. If discrepancies exist, the collaboration attempts to ascertain whether they arise from inadequacies in formation, conceptualization, or implementation.

An evaluation should incorporate four dimensions (Brewer & deLeon, 1983). The first is effectiveness, or the relationship between goals and actual results. The second is equity. Third, an evaluation measures adequacy of the efforts in order to determine if sufficient resources were delivered to solve the problem. Finally, an evaluation measures efficiency, an assessment of "how much bang for the buck."

Evaluations may take place at various levels. Weiss (1981) discusses three possible levels at which performance and expectations can be compared. The first is at the client level: Is service delivery improved as expected? The second focuses on the provider: Is the job easier? The third addresses the concerns of administrators and funders: Are costs reduced and waste eliminated?

Termination

Termination is the final phase in the development of a collaboration. Brewer and deLeon (1983) define termination as "the adjustment of policies and programs that have become dysfunctional, redundant, outmoded, unnecessary, or even counterproductive" (p. 385). Termination means that the collaboration as it has come to exist is ended, either as the result of successful resolution of the initial problem or, more typically, failure to achieve benefits that outweigh the costs.

Termination can also be thought of as a beginning. While a collaboration as it has come to be known ceases to operate, a new one may be developed from its roots. This may be accomplished by replacement of the old structure with a new one; consolidation of successful structures and elimination of outmoded ones; or the implementation of program adjustments to reflect the changing environment (Brewer & deLeon, 1983).

MEDIATING VARIABLES

Developmental stages are dramatically affected by an array of mediating variables that can hasten or halt a collaboration's efforts. In this section, we describe individual variables, drawing on the practical and theoretical literature that has been written about each. Because these variables affect collaborations in different ways, they are also considered "distinguishing characteristics" of collaborations.

Goals

In a collaboration, participants work to solve problems and advance a common vision or goal (Gray, 1989). Typically, the goal toward which the participants direct their efforts emanates from a mutually identified need that may arise from an external threat or an internal problem (Berkowitz, 1986; Caruso, 1981; Elder & Magrab, 1980; Jones & Stegelin, 1988; Lieberman, 1986; Reid, 1964; Reid & Chandler, 1976; Stafford et al., 1984; Wu, 1986). Regardless of the source, participants in a collaboration also believe that they cannot solve the problem individually (Drummond & Baker, 1974; Gray, 1985; Gray & Hay, 1986) because of resource scarcity or narrowness of problem conceptualization. In most collaborations, the coming together of the group serves the interests of both the collective and the individual participants (Black & Kase, 1963; Hord, 1986; Pareek, 1981; Stafford et al., 1984; Van de Ven, 1976), enabling them to engage in intensive joint planning and problem solving (Hord, 1985; Johnson et al., 1982; Lieberman, 1986; Stafford et al., 1984).

In any group, the successful identification of common goals is influenced by the initial level of agreement among members. Some groups may fully agree on goals from the beginning, pursuing "a desired state of affairs which the organization attempts to realize" (Etzioni, 1964, p. 6). More commonly, the formal goals adopted by the group are the product of many conflicting subgoals that are reconciled through consensual processes. Whether strategically handled through incremental negotiated planning or a series of iterative changes followed by evaluation, the process of bringing the group to agreement, to be most successful, must be handled without deference to the hierarchical ranking among participants. The real test of "good" goal decisions is that relevant interest groups will accept and work to implement them (Covey & Brown, 1985).

Achieving such consensus is not always simple, however. Sometimes it involves altering the scope and/or the nature of the collaboration's initial goals. Some groups, aware of the importance of maintaining consensus and achieving initial successes, select easily accomplishable goals at the outset, giving the collaboration the chance to build competence and cohesiveness. Later, when the collaboration is more solidly grounded, more comprehensive goals are established.

Goal consensus is further complicated and often constrained by organizational factors. In the private sector, management seeks to balance conflicting constituencies—shareholders, customers, employees, suppliers, debtors—each of whom holds a unique expectation of the company. Yet because the pursuit of profit normally takes precedence in the private sector, the demands of constituencies are relatively easily reconciled. In contrast, nonprofit and public-sector organizations are subservient to a board of directors and/or governmental guidelines, a fact that often restricts freedom of choice regarding the goals and operational strategies (Anthony & Young, 1984). In spite of some sector differences in achieving the task, there is no disagreement on the importance of common goals to the success of a collaboration.

Resources

In the previous chapter, the importance of scarce resources as a motivating variable for collaboration was discussed. In this section, attention is focused on the way in which available resources are shared and pooled as a mediator in the collaborative process. Sharing enables organizations to trade among themselves; for example, agency A contributes a commodity or a good to agency B in exchange for a service. In contrast, pooling allows all participants to contribute to the group. In spite of differences in sharing strategies, resource exchange is considered to have a profound influence on the collaborative effort (Dunkle & Nash, 1989; Flynn & Harbin, 1987; McNulty & Soper, 1983).

Although resources range from insufficient to plentiful, there is little agreement in the literature on the relationship between collaboration and the quantity of resources themselves. Some authors suggest that collaboration is based on the assumption that resources will be more abundant through sharing (Kraus, 1980), as in the case when parties have access to funds as a result of their collaborative efforts. Other writers warn that collaboration cannot create new resources but only make better use of existing ones (Weiss, 1981). In fact, some even suggest that collaborations represent a form of limited-resource management, and are thus a new means of coping with resource scarcity (Schindler-Rainman, 1981).

Because resource allocation is so fundamental to the collaborative process, numerous theories about the relationship between resources and collaborations, as well as numerous models for dealing with the issue of resource allocation, have emerged in the literature. In the exchange model, a lack of resources propels organizations to seek relationships, implying that organizations with fewer resources are more likely to enter into collaborations than those that are resource-rich (Martinson, 1982). Another perspective suggests that organizational interactions can be categorized on a continuum based on their method of resource sharing. At one end of the continuum are informal, or person-dependent, relationships, characterized by a lack of structure or resource pooling. At the other end are formalized organizational relationships, or even consolidation, in which a new entity is created out of the resources of the participants (Gamm, 1983; Intriligator, 1986). Variations in the center of the continuum include limited monetary or material contributions, use of a special program of one participant by another, and sharing of administrative capacities. Gamm (1983) labels the points on the continuum as social choice, coalition, confederative, federative, and unitary. Intriligator (1986) calls them person-dependent, contract, interorganizational relationship (IOR) administrative, and IOR collaborative.

Power and Authority

Not necessarily coercive, power relationships characterize any human endeavor, and collaborations are no exception. In practice, authority relations penetrate each stage and transaction in the collaborative process, from formation and conceptualization through implementation and evaluation to termination; they characterize, through formal and informal ties, the essential properties of the group (Flynn & Harbin, 1987; Intriligator, 1986). Some writers claim that the success of any collaborative effort is contingent on the effective resolution of natural authority issues (Gray, 1985; Gray & Hay, 1986; Kraus, 1980; Skaff, 1988; Stafford et al., 1984).

In a collaborative enterprise power emanates from many sources. Being an initiator of a collaboration is an important source of power. Conveners of voluntary collaborations hold enormous power because they select participants who, in turn, shape the identity of the group (Gray & Hay, 1986) and choose the goals and strategies by which the collaboration will function (Edgar & Maddox, 1983; Hord, 1985; O'Connell, 1985).

Another critical source of power is determined by who has access to or control over resources. As pointed out earlier, organizations lacking financial or other resources may be more likely to seek out collaborative relationships than those that are resource-rich. Beyond dollar resources, expertise, information, and access are potent sources of power within the collaborative relationship. An organization may possess recognized expertise about the issue at hand, may control part of the public policy process by virtue of previous connections, or may be in a position to oppose the project (Gray & Hay, 1986).

Beyond the existence of such resources, scholars note that power exists in relation to the availability of such resources to the collaboration. For example, Jacobsen and Cohen (1986) argue that resources are power only if an organization both controls them and is in the position to apply them to support or oppose a project. It appears that power hinges on both resource availability and utilization (actual or possible). Moreover, the degree of power accorded the resource holder is directly related to how much the collaborative players value the commodity and the degree to which the resource can be obtained from alternate "suppliers." If, for example, many individuals or groups can supply the resource, then its uniqueness—and consequently the power accorded its provider—is diminished (Skinner & Guiltinan, 1986).

Clearly, collaborative participants will hold different degrees of power. For example, one individual may have access to considerable knowledge resources but lack experience with policy-making procedures, a skill contributed by another individual. This reality fits distributive power theories that appear in the literature. Scholars suggest that beyond simple power sharing, in an ideal collaboration, the goal is *egalitarian* sharing of power and authority among the group members. Arguing that a top-down, hierarchical style of control is inappropriate in a collaborative setting, Gamm (1983) believes that power diffusion, not power elimination, is the ideal, and that it should be based on knowledge or expertise, not on role or function as in a bureaucracy. In other words, participants assume control over those activities for which they have expertise, but no single type of contribution is considered better or more powerful than any other. Despite the use of such measures as resources or expertise as the source of power, participants have equal authority. Consequently, leadership can be shared among participants according to the task at hand or it can be rotated so that no single agency or individual dominates the collaboration's work. While such equal distribution of power is difficult to achieve, it is the hallmark of a true collaboration: interorganizational relationships marked by large inequalities of power among participants are more accurately termed *coordinated efforts*.

This theoretical ideal of power distribution may be achieved in several ways. One is the division of tasks described above; another is the inclusion of those who will implement the decision in the decision-making process (Jones & Stegelin, 1988; Kraus, 1980; Van de Ven, 1976); and a third is the sharing of information via open communication among participants (Appley & Winder, 1977a; Hord, 1986; Kraus, 1980; Schaffer & Bryant, 1983; Trist, 1977).

Irrespective of which strategies are employed, developing trust among the participants is essential. De Bevoise (1986), in an insightful paper, reminds us of the importance of trust building when he points out that the term *collaboration* has as one of its meanings "cavorting with the enemy." Corroborating this formal definition, *Webster's Third International Dictionary* (1981) indicates that to collaborate is "to cooperate with or assist usually unwillingly an enemy of one's country." Coupling these definitions and the traditional competitive stance among organizations further underscores the importance of developing trust among collaborating parties if the ideal of an equitable sharing of power is to be realized (De Bevoise, 1986).

How well trust is achieved depends on perhaps the most important dimension of power and authority—the leadership of the collaboration. Virtually all the literature attests to the importance of a supportive, effective, flexible leader (Dunkle & Nash, 1989; Gans & Horton, 1975; Gray, 1985; McNulty & Soper, 1983; Schindler-Rainman, 1981; Wu, 1986). Yet leadership in a collaborative enterprise must be reconciled with the concepts of power sharing and leadership.

Typically, the roles of leaders are described as directive or facilitative. This categorization holds true whether the leader is internal or external to the group. The directive or controlling leader retains final authority and responsibility for the output of subordinates and thus has ultimate control in decision making (Turquet, 1974). Alternatively, a leader may be facilitative, assuming authority only as given by subordinates and delegating responsibility (and thereby power) for the final product to those who produce it.

The latter view is espoused most frequently in the literature on collaboration. Collaborative authority is created or sanctioned by those who empower it. The process of authorizing others builds conditions by which individual contributors can influence the group (Smith & Berg, 1987). Consonant with the theories of the geometric increase of power in a collaborative setting espoused by Kraus (1980), the process of empowering others increases the total amount of group and individual power (Smith & Berg, 1987).

The power of the collaboration emanates not only from the leadership but also from the authority lodged in the collaboration at the outset. Typically, collaborations are created in one of two ways: they may be fully voluntary or they may exist in response to a legal mandate (Gamm, 1981; Schopler, 1987; Trist, 1983; Warren, 1973; Weiss, 1981). A conceptual framework of group origin, structure, and outcome developed by Schopler (1987) dichotomizes the differences between voluntary and mandated groups. In a voluntary group, where group purpose and goals are shaped by the participants, power dynamics will be influenced by control over resources, expertise, and so on. The group will form more slowly, experience more conflict, and be less efficient, but group output is innovative and results in high member satisfaction. In a mandated group, one that is created to carry out a legislative mandate and whose purpose and tasks are specified by an external body, group relations will shift according to the control exerted by the outside agent. The group is more efficient and experiences fewer power struggles among the participants, but it yields a lower-quality output.

Writers disagree about the effects of mandates and authoritative third parties. On the positive side, some authors believe that mandates are the best insurance for obtaining effective participation (Cohen, 1989). Mandates may be a useful structural element if conditions are not conducive to collaboration (Gray, 1985), especially if conflict is high. A mandate can serve as a useful vehicle to help entities move from competitive to collaborative values (Appley & Winder, 1977b). On the negative side, required mandates may eliminate the vital group process of "mutual adjustment and concession" (Warren, 1973) or ideological consensus (Gray, 1985), or they may reduce the group's commitment to the task (Schopler, 1987). Federal- or state-level formal agreements, although necessary to bring order to an overlap of mandates, may still not work (Edgar & Maddox, 1983). As agencies seek to retain their autonomy, programs organized at higher levels may have little impact at the local level (Weiss, 1981) and may be less effective than grass-roots models (Edgar & Maddox, 1983).

As an addition or alternative to formal mandates, participants in collaborations often craft interagency agreements as a means of clarifying power and authority issues. These agreements can serve abstract and practical purposes, helping to focus, structure, and fund the activities (Olsen, 1983). In theory, an interagency agreement can be a highly effective mechanism for formalizing the relationships among participants in a collaboration. In practice, they are viewed as official commitments by each group to the joint effort (Intriligator, 1986). For example, the Kentucky Department of Education and the Cabinet for Human Resources identified a formal agreement, rather than a legal mandate or agency enthusiasm, as the first step in committing to an ongoing collaborative project (Hodges, 1987). An interagency agreement may also serve a critical role in the early resolution of conflict among the participants. Since participants must achieve consensus on the basic issues prior to drafting the agreement, conflict can be managed at the conceptualization rather than the implementation stage.

Interagency agreements generally focus on two major components: defining roles and responsibilities and identifying funding/resources. The former component is essential to the ongoing success of the collaboration, since the agreement defines boundaries and minimizes turf protection issues (Martinson, 1982; McNulty & Soper, 1983; Stafford et al., 1984; Wu, 1986). Some suggest that the clearer the role, the greater the agency commitment to the collaboration (Johnson et al., 1982). Interagency agreements have been particularly helpful in role clarification when often-ambiguous legislative mandates are implemented (Edgar & Maddox, 1983; Martinson, 1982; McNulty & Soper, 1983). The second component—resource specification—encourages participants to address questions of resource adequacy and commitments early on, thereby eliminating potential misunderstandings (Goldring, 1986; Schindler-Rainman, 1981).

Despite their importance and utility, interagency agreements are not without problems. Several authors suggest that such agreements give inadequate attention to the services to be provided to the target population (Bass, 1983; McNulty & Soper, 1983). This often means that the consumer is the last to recognize the shift in agency priorities. Others claim that agreements are forgotten once they are signed, rendering them ineffective for minimizing conflict or effecting real change. They may turn out to be little more than token efforts to fix existing system inadequacies (Bass, 1983).

As the federal government, states, and municipalities rush to pass mandates and encourage interagency agreements to collaborate, theorists will have more opportunity to study the relationship between mandates and the implementation of collaboration and to explore the effects of these mandates on collaboration at the service and system levels.

Flexibility

The fourth mediating variable or defining characteristic of a collaboration is the flexibility it accords itself and its members. Flexibility, as it is used in this context, means that the possibility for change exists at any time (Davidson, 1976; Flynn & Harbin, 1987; Fombrun, 1986; Hutinger, 1981; Trist, 1977). Other theorists label this concept with different words: Kraus (1980) uses the term organic to describe a collaborative structure that he defines as "fluid, adaptable and flexible," and Bennis (1966) calls the new system organic-adaptive, claiming that it will be temporary, rapidly changing, and constantly evolving in response to the problem. Whatever the nomenclature, the intent is clear: the flexibility of a collaboration both defines and influences the collaborative process.

Flexibility arises in response to both external and internal forces, characteristics of an uncertain environment where new structures are being created and old ones modified. Not only is the collaboration likely to influence such structures, but it can also alter the structure's mission or strategy. Changes in the environment may render the collaboration's activities outmoded or unnecessary (for example, a regulatory change may preclude the need for some of the work charted by the collaboration). Program beneficiaries may no longer need the services of the collaboration, or they may require expanded services. Flexibility enables collaborations to monitor and respond to the changing nature and scope of the problem.

Flexibility also permits participants to react to shifting boundaries among themselves and changing internal structures and role assignments. As the scope of the problem changes, new stakeholders who possess knowledge and expertise must be incorporated into the existing structure. As a consequence, the participants may assume new responsibilities or relinquish old ones. Internal changes experienced by a member organization or by the collaboration itself, such as staff turnover or funding growth, also necessitate a fluid organizational structure. Like any social collective, the framework of a collaboration must remain flexible, since its growth depends on the changing experiences of the participants (Fombrun, 1986; Hord, 1980; Stafford et al., 1984).

Just how collaborations manage their need for flexibility and the impact of such management on collaborative outcome have been debated in the literature. It suggests that as the group interacts and the environment changes, different structures and mechanisms for implementation must be developed and a model of interaction selected. Participants must understand which model is being used in order to minimize confusion and maximize success (Hord, 1985). And because the choice of a model is believed to impact on the outcome (Intriligator, 1986; Schopler, 1987), participants must be careful to select a model that allows for flexibility (Gamm, 1983; Intriligator, 1986).

The Odyssey of Collaboration in Early Care and Education

"**Odyssey:** . . . any long series of wanderings, especially when filled with notable experiences or hardships."

Random House College Dictionary, 1980

HAVING DISCUSSED THE MEANINGS and processes of collaboration, the remainder of this volume is devoted to its presence in the field of early care and education. Although collaborations are currently proliferating, there are endemic ideological and practical challenges that must be hurdled. To understand why the commitment to collaboration is emerging in the field with such fervor and what obstacles it faces, it is necessary to review the history of American early care and education. The following account emphasizes the periods, policies, and practices most germane to collaborative efforts in the field.

The evolution of American early care and education has been thoughtfully chronicled by many scholars (e.g., Beck, 1982; Billingsley & Giovannoni, 1972; Bremner, 1970–1974; Cahan, 1989; Fein & Clarke-Stewart, 1973; Grubb & Lazerson, 1982; Kahn & Kamerman, 1987; Lazerson, 1972; Marver & Larson, 1978; Mitchell, Seligson, & Marx, 1989; Steiner, 1976; Steinfels, 1973). A review of their studies suggests five recurring themes that shape this analysis.

1. From the earliest times, public attitudes toward early care and education were primarily framed by the hegemony of the home and the privacy/primacy of the family.
2. Because public values did not accord with out-of-home nonmaternal care, the financing of early care and education necessarily remained rooted primarily in the private sector.
3. Lacking public support and paling beside robust philanthropic and private-sector involvement, governmental commitments were episodic, half-hearted, and typically targeted to children and families

most in distress, thus permanently segregating both sponsorship (into public and private sectors) and participants (according to socioeconomic level).

4. When publicly sanctioned, early care and education efforts were handmaidens to widely divergent social missions, yielding a mixed array of governmental auspices and programs.

5. Ambiguity of purpose and inconsistency of commitment yielded a lack of precision and cogency in defining and executing federal-state relationships.

In short, ambiguity and inequity have characterized the development of highly segregated and fragmented services to America's young children.

THE EARLY YEARS

Any cogent history of early care and education must place the struggle *among* programs within the context of the struggle *for* them. Manifest in the development first of infant schools and then of day nurseries, the omnipresent value tug between home and nonmaternal care was prescient. Infant schools began as levers of moral reform, serving poor urban parents and children. Established in part to stave off social unrest, the schools provided personal and moral lessons for the children of the indigent and uneducated, providing what their parents could or did not. Services were also provided for the parents, enabling them to find employment while their children were removed "from the unhappy association of want and vice, and [were] placed under better influences" (Infant School Society of Boston, 1828). Serving those who could not help themselves, the infant schools were America's first efforts to alleviate poverty through education (Cahan, 1989). The effect, however, was "to establish poverty track educational institutions as practical alternatives to the traditional family-centered socialization process" (Tank, 1980, p. 16). Gradually, the infant school concept was extended to middle- and upper-income families on the premise that what was good for poor children might also benefit more advantaged youngsters (Beatty, 1981, cited in Cahan, 1989). But such efforts were short-lived owing to the reemergence, beginning in the 1830s, of the Puritan ethic that emphasized the importance of maternal care.

The course of early care and education in our country was seeded in the brief life of the infant schools. Herein lay clear manifestations of early tensions between home and out-of-home services—dubbed the "domestic ethic" (Cahan, 1989). These tensions, illustrative of the first theme discussed above, partially accounted for the demise of the infant schools. No less apparent in this period were deep-seated ideological differences that yielded our income-segregated system of services. And finally, lack of public commitment to the infant schools is corroborated by the fact that they remained within the private sector, almost fully funded by philanthropists. Thus by the 1840s, the second theme had emerged, and fragmentation as a structural variable of early care and education was firmly entrenched.

If fragmentation was ensconced early on, it became even more prominent with the rise in popularity of day nurseries and nursery schools in the late nineteenth and early twentieth centuries. Lacking an organized system of care, nineteenth-century parents resorted to a variety of arrangements. History indicates that mothers took their children to work (particularly those women who were employed as domestics); fathers stayed home with the children, thus "split-shifting" caretaking responsibilities; relatives and friends were commandeered into service; or children were simply left alone. Dissatisfied with this situation, philanthropists—largely via religious and charitable organizations—came to the rescue. Day nurseries grew as "an explicit response to the problems surrounding the competing demands of maternal employment and child care for the children of the poor" (Cahan, 1989, p. 15). Under the careful nurturance of women activists, individual day nurseries opened throughout metropolitan areas. In an attempt to promote high standards, some of the day nurseries joined together to form the National Federation of Day Nurseries in 1898.

From their inception, the day nurseries had multiple intentions and offered a variety of services. In an effort to stave off the institutionalization of poor children, many of the day nurseries attempted to provide broader social services, such as counseling parents, providing job placements, and offering training. Some hospital-based programs offered health and nutritional services. Although funds were tight and quality questionable, the day nurseries clearly offered more than moral instruction; they became one component of an embryonic social welfare system, legitimizing the purview of multiple domains over the care and education of America's young.

As happened in the case of the infant schools, when concern about poor children mounts, it is often accompanied by renewed interest in all children. Learning from German immigrants who brought with them Froebel's teachings, practitioners became interested in the concept of the kindergarten, which brought additional early care and education players onto the scene. Distinguished from the day nurseries, the kindergartens stressed education and served primarily children from educated, well-to-do families. The onset of a major depression (1873–1877) inspired philanthropists to create free kindergartens for the children of the needy, thus accelerating kindergarten expansion. It was hoped that, like the day nurseries, the kindergartens would adopt a broader mission that would include nutrition, cleanliness, and good health and work habits (Ross, 1976). Unable to accommodate the needs of all children, financial supporters pressed for public support and free kindergarten associations were organized—apparently with success, because by the end of the century, over half of all kindergartens were operated by public schools (Kahn & Kamerman, 1987).

The rise of public kindergartens has left three legacies germane to collaboration. First, while half the kindergartens were in schools, the other half were distributed among numerous sponsors, including churches, labor unions, temperance groups, private businesses, and settlement houses, thereby fortifying the mixed-delivery system as a permanent characteristic of early care and education in this country. Second, as this great variety of institutions began to serve young children, the fairly coherent ideology of an earlier time gave way to the varying goals and norms of the host institutions. For example, kindergartens in schools became more structured and formal, probably opening the door for the progressive movement that was to follow, and programs in churches took on a religious patina. Diversification of host settings was accompanied by diversification in pedagogy and curriculum, prevalent until fairly recently. Third, the kindergarten movement predicted the historic response of government regarding the care and education of young children—reactive, partial, and regarded as a means to a greater social end, the last being the reform of urban school systems, which were already deemed "corrupt and inefficient" (Mitchell et al., 1989). As such, the kindergarten movement reinforced inconsistent delivery systems—the third theme—and demonstrated that even early on, services to young children took root as part of a broader social agenda—the fourth theme.

THE TURN OF THE CENTURY

As the twentieth century dawned, still without consistent federal involvement in early care and education, systemic and ideological fragmentation prevailed. The day nurseries, assailed by resurgent concerns about maternal employment and nonmaternal care, began to differentiate the "worthy" from the "unworthy" poor in choosing whom to serve. With this designation came greater stigmatization of those in the day nurseries and the nurseries themselves. They were looked on simply as a temporary aid to troubled families, rather than a just claim of working women.

This perspective signaled the demise of the day nurseries and ushered in a greater role for government in the care and education of the nation's youngsters. Given the first theme—ideological aversion to out-of-home nonmaternal care—it is not surprising that mothers' pensions, a social invention to keep women in the home, were devised. Representing an early form of public assistance, the pensions enabled children to remain in their homes and sanctioned the mother's importance as the primary caregiver. By 1919, 39 states plus Alaska and Hawaii had passed legislation allocating such pensions, but the pensions were not ubiquitous (Cahan, 1989). Because the legislation made the pensions optional at local discretion, some states and localities refused to endorse them, leaving the patchwork array of supports that was emerging as a defining characteristic of early care and education. The ambiguous purpose of the law and the inconsistent commitment at various levels of government set the stage for the lack of precision and cogency in defining and executing federal-state relationships that was to hallmark future efforts—the fifth theme.

PROFESSIONALISM AND PHILANTHROPY

Various rationales have been offered for the rise of another player in the field, the American nursery school. Among them are the demise of the neighborhood following World War I; a perceived decline in the capacity of the family to socialize its young; the advent of urbanization and congested living conditions that deprived children of play space; and the desire of mothers to provide their children with extrafamilial opportunities for regular socialization. Though each rationale holds some measure of truth, perhaps the greatest impetus for the growing nursery school movement was the confluence of an emerging child-study movement, professionalism, and the support that rendered them both effective—philanthropy.

From World War I through the 1930s, child psychology and the child-study movement had a profound impact on service delivery to young children and their families. With assistance from the Laura Spelman Rockefeller Memorial Foundation, child-study institutes were established at several colleges and universities. In addition to generating research, the institutes established nursery schools as laboratories for their work, as did many colleges and universities. Lessons garnered were transmitted to other nursery schools that had emerged since roughly 1915. In contrast to the day nurseries, most nursery schools were part-day and served children of middle- and upper-class families, reinforcing, yet again, the income segregation of preschool-aged youngsters.

Despite comparative segregation, the impact of the child-study and nursery movements was felt by the day nurseries and other organizations serving poor children. Drawing on a growing body of literature and effective models of quality early childhood programs, the day nurseries refined their visions of quality and sought to emulate the nursery schools pedagogically and practically. Unfortunately, limited funds prohibited the majority of day nurseries from rising to desired performance levels, and the controversy over developmental versus custodial care came into question, resurfacing the two-tiered question, this time without innuendo. With sad clarity, income segregation became synonymous with quality segregation. Low-income children received low-quality services; high-income children, high-quality services.

THE FEDERAL GOVERNMENT TAKES THE PLUNGE—HALTINGLY

Motivated by the ravages of the Great Depression and President Franklin D. Roosevelt's commitment to offer the American people a New Deal, Congress authorized for the first time funds to establish nursery schools. Brought about primarily by a need to provide jobs for unemployed workers, 3,000 nursery schools opened quickly, serving an estimated 65,000 children and employing between 6,000 and 8,000 adults. Despite the avowed adult raison d'être for the Depression emergency nursery schools, they were to embody the emerging knowledge regarding the delivery of comprehensive and quality services to young children—at least in theory. In practice, the schools placed their first priority on meeting children's health and nutritional needs in order to spare them the devastating effects of malnutrition and hunger. Because funds were limited and priorities clear, most of the Depression emergency schools were not of high quality. In another related event, Title V of the Social Security Act of 1935 provided support for child welfare (including child care) and research.

Interestingly, the federal government's first foray into the field set several precedents and clearly set in stone the themes discussed above. First, there was a great (and prescient) dichotomy between what the government hoped would be delivered and what it actually supported. Second, because funds for the programs were funneled through the Federal Emergency Relief Agency (FERA), supported by input from the Children's Bureau, the command center for the program was out of the hands of educators or child developmentalists. This was not the form of collaboration detailed in the previous chapter, but it mitigated the cooperation and coordination between professions necessary to provide effective care and education for young children. Moreover, its administrative structure at the federal level signaled the low priority accorded children and children's agencies and firmly reinforced the federal-level fragmentation of children's services—the fortification of theme 3. And as if fragmentation were not bad enough, it should be noted that the Farm Security and Federal Housing Administrations also ran day-care programs. Third, because of ambiguity in the way dollars flowed to municipalities, the federal-state-local conundrum was reinforced (theme 5). Finally, the act was significant in that many of the "nursery" schools were housed in public schools and provided full-time care, perhaps the first widespread acknowledgment of the isomorphic relationship between care and education.

Egged on by another national crisis, World War II, the federal government entered the child-care arena again under the aegis of the Community Facilities (Lanham) Act administered by the Federal Works Administration (FWA)—FERA's successor. Never fully sympathetic to the use of Lanham Act money for child care, the FWA was dubbed an agency "that never ceased to look ahead to termination of the program" (Steiner, 1976, p. 17), a blatant acknowledgment of the federal government's tenuous commitment to early care and education.

To be eligible for funds, child-care centers in war-impacted areas were considered public works. Note that contrary to the conventional wisdom that frequently accords the Lanham Act "model" status, it did not provide a truly national system of care. Moreover, though estimates of the number of children served in the centers vary from 105,000 to 1.6 million (Steiner, 1976), there can be no doubt that only a fraction of needy youngsters were enrolled (Cahan, 1989).

Part of the enrollment difficulty shaped several legacies of federal involvement in child care. It has been suggested that many eligible communities did not apply for Lanham Act funds because federal requirements (for matching funds and return of unused dollars at the end of the fiscal year) made operations untenable. Those who did apply faced a federal nightmare involving no fewer than seven federal agencies. Though the Lanham Act attempted to establish federal-state cooperative arrangements, the lines of authority were very unclear; although it provided for direct grants to local communities, the guidelines recommended that the Office of Education or the Children's Bureau—both of which had strong state ties—approve the programs. Despite efforts by both these agencies to control child-care services, they remained the responsibility of the War Department. Rather predictably, interagency rivalries became the norm because mediating variables of collaboration (mutual goals, resource and power sharing, and flexibility) were never resolved. Further, reminiscent of past history, once funds were provided they were insufficient to render a quality program. In some cases, communities were able to significantly augment their Lanham Act dollars, fostering better services.

Without doubt, the Lanham Act effort confirmed the national ethos toward child care—one of intervention to meet a greater social cause. But in exacerbating systemic fragmentation, intergovernmental confusion, and jurisdictional conflict, it made an indelible imprint. What could have been merely idiosyncratic events during the New Deal were becoming permanent, if not defining, characteristics of our nation's approach to early care and education. For all effective purposes, the Lanham Act made fragmentation an inevitability.

ADDITIONAL FEDERAL EFFORTS

Following World War II, the common belief was that life would return to "normal," with men assuming their roles as breadwinners and women theirs as homemakers. It was anticipated that there would no longer be a need for federally supported child care, legitimating the closing of the Lanham Act centers in 1946. Children, well tended by at-home mothers, could benefit from the rapidly expanding public half-day kindergartens. Even the Korean War did not lead to rekindled enthusiasm for child care. In essence, despite some proposed "Cold War" day-care bills offered by Senator Jacob Javits, the decade and a half between the end of World War II and the Kennedy administration was void of serious federal attention to child care or early education. President John Kennedy's desire to expand child-care services for working mothers was manifest in a message to Congress, followed by proposed legislation and a supplemental appropriation of

$800,000 in 1963, the first federal financial assistance for child care since 1946.

Enthusiasm for young children resurfaced in policy guise in the 1960s when a confluence of civil rights, education, and employment legislation led to the development of the nation's Head Start program, the 1967 amendments to the Social Security Act, and a host of additional child-related acts. Establishing a completely new funding apparatus and a structure that bypassed the states, Head Start was bred of mixed parentage—the Office of Child Development and the Office of Economic Opportunity. But hardly a better marriage existed. Through it, millions of children and families have been served, a national research laboratory was conceived, and employment and training for countless personnel (many of them poor mothers) rendered. Nonetheless, Head Start remained programmatically isolated from other early care and education efforts, despite a strong commitment to link it with health and social service providers in order to enhance direct services offered to children and families.

Head Start, though the most widely recognized, was not the only legacy of federal intervention in early care and education in the 1960s. While day care for children of welfare recipients had been a part of the Social Security Act since 1962, the 1967 amendments significantly broadened its authorization (Jackson, 1973). Titles IV-A (Aid to Families with Dependent Children) and IV-B (Child Welfare Services) were an uncapped source of funds for child care for low-income families, and Title IV-C (Work Incentive Program) provided funding to place adult welfare recipients in jobs or job training and to subsidize child care to make their employment possible.

Funding from the federal government also came via education in the form of the Elementary and Secondary Education Act (ESEA) of 1965, which permitted dollars to be used for, among other things, preschool services for low-income children. Title VII of the Housing and Urban Development Act provided support for child-care centers, and the Model Cities legislation permitted day-care expenditures amounting to about $9 million in 1971. Community Action Programs included provisions for preschool and child-care services. Community Health Centers under National Institutes of Mental Health allowed for construction funds to be used for child-care centers. Department of the Interior funds for American Indians were also available for child care.

The mélange of efforts created in the mid to late 1960s yielded greatly increased services for low-income children and their families, to be sure. But less well understood, the proliferation of early care and education activity during this era also marked a historical turning point with significant consequences for the system. Contradicting past practice, these federal involvements were to endure beyond any other national efforts launched to that time. Despite precarious funding levels and a number of attempts—some successful—to sweep away the enactments of the era, the 1960s efforts secured a permanent place in the federal pocketbook for the non-school-based programs for young children. Unlike the comparatively short-lived Depression nurseries or Lanham Act child-care efforts, Head Start, ESEA, and Title XX (the social services title of the Social Security Act) became enduring components of the early care and education landscape.

Such commitment marked a turning point not only for the federal government but also for the private sector. Private philanthropy and religious and charitable organizations that played such a pivotal role in contouring the early care and education system were joined by a new and powerful player—the federal government. More robust public involvement was accompanied by uncertainty in the private sector. Independent for-profit providers wondered if they would lose some of their clientele and worried that more government involvement would mean more government regulation. Whatever the specific programmatic or regulatory results, efforts of the 1960s and 1970s realigned the face of American early care and education, broadening it from a matter of private interest to one of significant public *and* private concern.

These policy changes were reflective of a marginal (and temporary) shift in ideology as well, one having to do with the first theme noted so often in this volume. To this point in history, early care and education had been captive to national ambivalence regarding non-maternal care. Although new federal commitments did not mean that confusion was eliminated, they did affirm that women—particularly low-income women—could be effective in dual roles as parent and worker. Further, with credibility augmented by early scholarly work regarding the nature of intelligence, an enthusiasm for the importance of the early years resurfaced. Reflective of earlier eras and characteristic of the reform spirit in general, unbridled optimism posited that even modest interventions could go a long way in stemming poverty, compensating for "cultural deficits," and enhancing the life chances of poor children and their parents.

Such policy and ideological changes brought with them pervasive, though not necessarily unpredictable, practical consequences. First, as preschool education was increasingly extended to the poor, the income segregation that had characterized earlier efforts was fortified, rendering the third theme—income segregation of children—an immutable factor of early care and education. Although Head Start made provisions for the enrollment of 10 percent nonpoor children, and some Title XX efforts used a voucher mechanism, federally subsidized services remained the province of the poor, while middle- and upper-income children were enrolled in separate programs. Clearly, federal efforts altered *who* paid but not *how* or *where* rich and poor children were served.

Second, the involvement of multiple federal agencies with scattered responsibilities abetted an already badly fragmented delivery system. At the federal level, there was a lack of clarity regarding the relationships among the agencies that had responsibility for early care and education programs. Congress questioned whether the Office of Economic Opportunity (OEO) should operate and plan programs for the poor and why there should be different kinds of programs emerging in OEO and Health, Education and Welfare (HEW). The Children's Bureau, initially created to "investigate and report on all matters pertaining to the welfare of children and child life among all classes of our people" (Bremner, 1970–1974, p. 774), was perceived as "dinky, depressed, uninspired and uninspiring" (Steiner, 1976, p. 39), certainly not up to the task of coordinating early care and education strategies or policies.

Soon thereafter, the lack of coordination and clarity at the federal level manifested itself at state and local levels. Administratively, limited federal cohesion resulted in the proliferation of program-specific (and highly uncoordinated) guidelines and regulations. Often quickly promulgated and confusing, the plethora of guidelines left states and locales with the job of ferreting out which funds could and should be used for which discrete services. In some states, rules governing the use of matching funds (particularly apparent in Title IV-A) were in conflict with state laws. Other states, even those better able to deal with regulatory and legal conflicts, became hesitant partners, fearful that they would be quickly asked to assume responsibility for federal commitments of ambiguous duration. The fifth theme of poor relations between various levels of government herein became a more powerful determinant—or detriment—in early care and education.

With the appearance of fiscal flexibility, guidelines often offered hope to local managers. But the common phrase, "funds *may* be used for . . ." was frequently dismissed in reality. Co-mingling program dollars or allowing families flexibility of choice was prohibited. For example, children funded under Work Incentives Program (WIN) dollars could not be mixed with children receiving Model Cities funds, even if the programs were nearer the children's homes or more convenient for their families (Jackson, 1973). Left to their own ingenuity, local agencies were charged with creating a coherent mosaic out of hundreds of ill-fitting pieces. So difficult was the dilemma that Jackson reported that "the extent and quality of actual services may depend more on the competence of local agencies and groups to thread the maze than on the local communities' desire for child care services" (p. 42). Localities that succeeded were those that were able to build any of the tiers of cooperation, coordination, or collaboration among agencies.

The extent of the fragmentation had several direct consequences for child-care accessibility, quality, and supply. Accessibility was hampered by several factors. First, child-care programs funded from different sources were often forced to compete with one another for children who fell into their prescribed income and geographic restrictions while other youngsters, only fractionally different, went unserved. Second, because of systemic complexity and because there were so few efforts to inform parents of their options, many who would have benefited from services were simply unaware of available programs.

Quality was hampered because dedicated providers, attempting to administer programs, manage facilities, and provide support to staff and parents, were often diverted from these duties to maneuver through the early care and education funding and regulatory maze. Uncoordinated regulations meant that providers expended countless hours meeting the multiple and inconsistent sets of standards imposed by local, state, and/or federal agencies. Patching together grants demanded constant attention by facile providers, often discouraging even the most competent professionals from the field.

Finally, the complexity of the process threatened equitable distribution of supply. The most technically competent and politically adept providers were favored in a highly competitive process (Keyserling, 1972). Often, success begot success, so that more sophisticated providers took on increasingly greater shares of the market, edging out smaller providers and smaller programs.

A kind interpretation of the fragmentation and chaos generated during this period suggests that government was simply overzealous and naive. More skeptical analysis suggests that the ambiguity was rooted in more general questions of value and structure. On the value issue, a plausible explanation is that recalling earlier eras, government felt the programs would be short-lived; consequently there was no need to expend valuable time or resources to create a stable and integrated infrastructure. On the structural issue, it is possible that early care and education, as it grew in the federal domain, simply fell prey to ongoing federalist concerns. Largely unresolved, the question of the balance of power between federal and state government must be reexplored by each generation. This era and these efforts were no exception. Irrespective of rationale, an ill-coordinated, cumbersome, and entangled delivery system was the product of decades of history.

CHAPTER 6

Rectifying the Problems: Calls to Collaborate

"The Task Force believes that when collaboration among early child-hood programs does not occur, programs often compete for limited resources and staff, as well as for children and families. On the other hand, collaborative efforts can facilitate joint planning for staff development, and provide continuity for children and families . . . collaborative networks can provide a strong voice for increasing needed resources for early childhood programs."

National Association of State
Boards of Education, 1989

As THE PROGRAMS OF THE 1960s burgeoned, the pervasiveness of systemic problems quickly became apparent. By the early 1970s, both the executive and legislative branches of government recognized collaboration's potential, seeing it as a strategy that could help redress the fragmentation and inequity that pervaded the early care and education field.

EARLY FEDERAL INITIATIVES TO COORDINATE SERVICES

In December 1967, Congress amended the Economic Opportunity Act (Section 522[d]) and called upon the secretary of Health, Education and Welfare and the director of the Office of Economic Opportunity to "take all necessary steps to coordinate programs under their jurisdiction which provide day care so as to attain, if possible, a common set of program standards and regulations and mechanisms for coordination at the State and local level" (National Academy of Sciences, 1972,

p. 1). Shortly thereafter, in April 1968, the White House proposed a Federal (Interagency) Panel on Early Childhood with responsibility to improve all early childhood programs financed by federal funds. More explicitly, its purpose was to develop plans for the most effective use of child-care funds for operation, research, training, and technical assistance available to each of the federal departments and agencies.

The Community Coordinated Child Care (4C) Effort

To carry out the charge of Congress, the Federal Panel on Early Childhood established the Community Coordinated Child Care Program (4C), the first federally initiated effort to coordinate early care and education. Originally, the vision was to establish mechanisms within communities that would link all the programs—profit, private nonprofit, and government nonprofit—with the goal of promoting coordination, cutting waste, and improving the scope and quality of services within the community. The intent was not to completely integrate all programs (although this was not prohibited) but rather to engender cooperative efforts by sharing services and staff, engaging in joint cross-agency training and visitations, and establishing common programs whereby responsibility could be shared across sites.

Over the next 6 months, efforts to publicize and promote the 4C initiative took place. The Day Care and Child Development Council (DCCDC) was hired to provide technical assistance; the Federal Panel created the Standing Committee on 4C to formulate strategies for the coordination of the programs; regional representatives were named to Federal Regional 4C Committees (the regional counterparts to the Standing Committee), which were to select pilot locations; and guidelines for the pilots were developed. By August 1969, 24 project sites (8 states, 14 communities, and 2 national pilots) had been established. By October 1969, a central 4C office had been set up in Washington as a division of the Office of Child Development and pilot nominations had been received. The functions of this rather elaborate governmental apparatus were to assist state and local bodies on organizational, funding, and system delivery matters.

The concept rapidly gained visibility and popularity, so that by August 1971, 278 active 4Cs had been formally recognized. Recognition meant that a 4C was a functional coordinating body with an approved plan and certification from the Federal Regional 4C Committee. Despite some reservations, many communities organized 4Cs, motivated in part by the hidden promise of obtaining federal funds.

But before windfalls cascaded on communities, 4Cs had to be

operational, a demanding undertaking. Except for a few that were
able to commandeer local foundation support and the federal pilots
(each of which received an average of $9,000 the first year), most 4Cs
spent considerable time obtaining start-up and operational dollars.
Because funds were scarce and often insufficient to meet needs, 4Cs
often lodged themselves within extant community organizations and
then found it difficult to establish their independence later. Some 4Cs
that were unable to obtain funds disbanded, but others became re-
markably successful. By the fall of 1971, each of at least six 4Cs was
administering sums of money exceeding $1 million annually (National
Academy of Sciences, 1972). More typically, however, 4Cs attempted
to draw on Model Cities and Title IV-A funds, although these options
were hardly problem-free.

Just as the financial picture of individual 4C efforts was idiosyncratic, so too were their functional characteristics and activities. Some
4Cs became committees under larger community organizations, some
within public and some within private agencies. Many became independent associations, and others, particularly those at the state level,
were linked to state government. Some elected to operate programs,
while others assumed planning, coordination, public information,
training, staff development, and advocacy functions. Given these
widespread differences, the 4C initiative provides a natural laboratory
for investigating the process and outcome of collaborative experiences.

The common perception is that the 4C program was modestly
successful, at best. Steiner sums up the sentiment well: "Most attention was paid to coordinating matters of little importance probably
because matters of great importance like day care program standards
are inherently too divisive to permit coordination" (1976, p. 48). Critical of the DCCDC's final report, Steiner adds: "Accomplishments
were measured not by services provided to the target populations nor
by new ideas generated, nor by resources made available on behalf of
a stated objective, but by a count of formal organizations created to
fulfill an unspecified task" (p. 50).

Such dissatisfaction was confirmed by Morgan (1972), who attributed much of the problem to the "conflict between Washington and
the regional offices" (p. 7). Not only did the tensions delay implementation of the concept for months, but significant problems arose because the guidelines displayed no understanding of the very different
roles that local and state 4C committees should have had. Training
efforts, initially robust, were watered down, a dilemma exacerbated

by the fact that the "selection of pilots was arbitrary, by criteria which [were] very unclear" (Morgan, 1972, p. 9). In addition to concerns regarding the federal and regional structure, other questions surfaced as to whether an operating agency could or should become a coordinating agency.

With speculation about the value of the 4C program mounting, the prestigious National Academy of Sciences was asked to conduct an assessment of the program, the primary national assessment conducted by nonparticipants. More benign than the Steiner analysis but reflecting the Morgan concerns, the evaluation concluded that "4C represents . . . a sound concept as far as it went and one which, had it been properly implemented, might have made a major contribution" (National Academy of Sciences, 1972, p. 32).

Highly critical of the role of the federal government, the report levies complaints of inadequate federal-level staff from the outset, little federal-level coordination, underutilization of the Federal Panel on Early Childhood, poor communications to regional offices, poor functioning of the Federal Regional (Interagency) Committees, little top-level and national office support from the Office of Child Development, and, not unpredictably, insufficient resources. Note that resolution of each of these items is imperative for successful collaboration. Report recommendations were caught in the midst of significant legislative child-care initiatives (discussed below), preventing the panel from predicting the precise statutory framework within which the recommendations should fall.

Nonetheless, the intent was clear. The panel recommended that the federal government should encourage and give support to cooperative efforts: "For the federal government to abandon its role in this area would seriously set back such coordinative efforts as have emerged and are, in a significant number of communities, proving effective" (National Academy of Sciences, 1972, p. 41). In recommending a new approach, the panel firmly endorsed the need for collaborative structures and for local control within the framework of governmental policy. Specifically, the panel took a bold step forward by recommending that

> a small portion of *all* federal funds for child care, pre-school educational and related programs and services be earmarked by appropriate legislative or administrative action for allocation to those states, urban counties, and cities that establish in their governmental structure an Office of Child Development, or its equivalent, as an intragovernmental mechanism for the *coordination of the full range of child care and development, early*

education and related health and family service programs. (p. 42; emphasis
added)*

The lessons from 4Cs are sadly reminiscent of other federal efforts in the field. Like the day nurseries and the Lanham Act, the 4C
initiative was a federal response to broad social problems that was
inadequately funded to accomplish its stated mission and was cur-
tailed prematurely before its benefits could be fully realized. The difference was one of magnitude, on two fronts. The 4C effort was not a
response to a major national crisis; rather it was essentially a within-
field response to a problem deeply but not widely felt by the American public. Constituent support was limited and so was funding, the
second difference in magnitude. The 4C vision, like that of other
demonstration efforts to follow, set out to reform a system with woefully inadequate funds and governmental supports. Its placement in
the Children's Bureau, never established to operate programs, was an
organizational error; the allocation of too few dollars to meet too many
expectations, a strategic error. Attempting the nearly impossible, the
4C effort was destined for failure from the outset. But ironically, despite 4Cs' general lackluster performance programmatically, it was an
idea whose time had come. Coordinating early care and education
was a tenacious concept, one that was to resurface frequently in somewhat different guises during the 1970s and 1980s.

Comprehensive Child Development Act of 1971

The degree to which the Comprehensive Child Development Act of
1971 attended to coordination and collaboration is debatable. A curso-
ry review of the bill indicates some sensitivity to the need for collaboration. At the federal level, the bill required the secretary of Health,
Education and Welfare to direct the Office of Child Development and
the Office of Education to promulgate joint regulations to achieve
coordination. Further, the secretary was authorized to prescribe appropriate regulations and arrangements to ensure coordination between the Social Security program's aid and service arrangements
and the Comprehensive Child Development Program.

Throughout the long negotiations, the twin issues of delivery

---

*A nearly verbatim recommendation appeared in the report of the National Coun-
cil of Jewish Women, *Windows on Day Care*, with the word *all* highlighted (Keyserling,
1972, p. 226). The pivotal position of Mary Keyserling in both these efforts should be
noted.

mechanisms and control framed much of the debate. With child advocate Marian Wright Edelman leading the way, a legion of organizations and individuals pressed for local control of the programs. Their efforts yielded a system of prime sponsors—units established to administer the effort. Each prime sponsor was required to establish Child Development Councils (CDCs) that would (1) serve as a means of coordinating and integrating service to children within the prime sponsor area; (2) ensure programs established under the act met standards of quality established by the secretary; and (3) ensure that funds authorized were equitably distributed. Augmenting the work of the CDCs, Local Policy Councils were to be responsible for determining child development needs in their areas and approving project applications and program statements.

Despite these efforts, some contended that the legislation did not go far enough. Critics asserted that the prime sponsors should have become focal points for all federally supported child care, including Model Cities, Department of Labor, and Social Security Act programs. Without such a provision, child care would continue to proliferate different eligibility and funding structures, segregate children, discourage potential suppliers, and dampen the vitality of the day-care sector (Nelson & Young, 1973).

Controversy regarding the legislation did not rest solely in the academic community. Despite passage of the act in the House and Senate (only to be felled by presidential veto), there was much debate on Capitol Hill. Dubbed an administrative monstrosity by some, an irresponsible promise by others, the legislation evoked lingering concern over the local control issue. Offering a "realistic and practical" alternative, Representatives Quie, Dellenback, Hansen, and Steiger introduced H.R. 13649, which provided an interim solution focused on program consolidation and coordination. The substitute bill posited that all child-care or child development programs carried on or assisted by the United States should be administered, to the maximum extent feasible, by a single federal agency.

It is our intention that as coordination efforts begin to emerge that recipients of Federal monies would not have to write individual applications going to five, ten, or even fifteen individual agencies to receive funds, but that there may emerge a simplified mechanism for applying for money as well as dispensing money. In this way, we see competition and rivalry between programs hopefully being eliminated and concentrated efforts directed on behalf of children. (U.S. House of Representatives, 1972, p. 50)

Thus a commitment to coordination, though not a strong one, made itself heard via the Comprehensive Child Development Act. Because of the Nixon veto, no one can know how such efforts might have fared. But a clear consequence of the veto was a diminution of advocacy for child-care efforts in general and for collaborative efforts in particular.

Legislative Efforts of 1975 and 1979

The Child and Family Services Act of 1975, sponsored by Walter Mondale and John Brademas, was another attempt to extend a federal commitment to young children and their families. This act would have provided $1.8 billion for planning, developing, establishing (including training and technical assistance), maintaining, and operating a variety of child and family service programs (Mitchell, Seligson, & Marx, 1989). Comprehensive services would have been offered to preschool children in the greatest need. Though not particularly robust, commitment to collaboration took two forms: First, programs could be operated by an array of agencies, including the public schools and private nonprofit agencies; second, to coordinate the resources and services, the bill called for the creation of a Child and Family Services Coordinating Council. But, again, there was no opportunity to test the efficacy of the councils because the bill, like the Comprehensive Child Development Act before it, was brought down by strident charges regarding the professionalization of parenting and the "Sovietization" of America's children.

No less satisfactory was the result of Senator Alan Cranston's Child Care Act of 1979. Designed to assist working parents, this legislation proposed direct funding to the states. Short-lived because it lacked strong support from members of the Carter administration and the child-care advocacy community (Levine, 1982), not to mention others, the bill was withdrawn prior to a vote.

Collectively, these three unsuccessful legislative attempts cast a pall over child care as a salable issue, particularly given a new and more conservative Congress, as Beck (1982) has noted. Nevertheless, despite the uncertainty of the times, the need for coordination remained strong. Growing numbers of working women, the sheer numbers of children in need of supplementary care, and the "demands for a conscious family policy" were all motivating forces for a more coherent approach (Grubb & Lazerson, 1982, p. 217). But from where would it come?

RESOURCE AND REFERRAL PROGRAMS: A HOPE FOR COHERENCE

Not waiting for a federal imprimatur, isolated communities throughout the nation set about the challenging task of making child-care arrangements more coherent through the development of information and referral systems (I&Rs). Because the I&Rs developed independently, often at great geographic distances from one another, and with different roots, their specific services varied widely and were tailored to individual community needs. Despite their individuality, most I&Rs attempted to provide parents with information about available services in the community. They served as initial points of contact with the child-care system for parents, many of whom were justifiably confused about availability, quality, and access to service. As well as helping parents locate care, some I&Rs helped to stimulate supply by providing technical assistance to new programs and family day-care homes; many worked to upgrade the quality of programs by providing staff training and establishing employee clearinghouses for those wishing to enter the field; and some developed rich databases that were later useful for significant advocacy efforts.

The I&R movement represents the root of the collaborative tradition in early care and education. As the first sustained collaborative effort, it is the base from which all collaborative activities are taking place today. By recounting its history in some detail, we may gain a practical understanding of the process by which collaboration unfolds, the structure it takes, and the mediating variables that affect it.

Actual starting dates of the I&R efforts are not easy to pinpoint. Levine (1982) suggests that the concept of information and referral has been a component of social service delivery since the 1870s, when the "charity organization movement gave birth to the social service exchange, a type of coordinating body designed to increase access to and reduce duplication of human services" (p. 388). Alfred Kahn's (1966) work on the British Citizen's Advice Bureaus, which laid the groundwork for the Alliance of Information and Referral Services, was no doubt seminal in the growth of the American movement. These efforts, coupled with the fact that some I&Rs were direct outgrowths of the 4C projects, could lead observers to date the beginning of the movement to the 1960s (Kahn & Kamerman, 1987). In her historical analysis of I&Rs, Siegel (1983) noted that "the past year marked the tenth anniversaries of many of the original child care information and referral agencies" (p. 2), suggesting that some of the pioneer services postdated the 1960s.

Regardless of the precise date of launch, the momentum for I&R picked up considerably in the 1970s with the help of Ford Foundation funding, which provided support for the first national I&R network meeting and for some individual programs. (It should be noted that the Ford Foundation also supported Kahn's work, thereby underscoring the importance of private philanthropy in the national history of collaboration.) Though critical to later success, foundation support was not the only accelerator of the I&R concept: research, buttressed by strong ideological support for parental choice, stimulated the momentum for I&Rs. Certain about the positive effects of early intervention, the research was ambiguous about any preferred delivery mode, leading noted scholars to advocate for mixed-delivery systems and/or parental choice (Clarke-Stewart, 1977; Larson, 1975; Skerry, 1978; Woolsey, 1977; Zigler & Hunsinger, 1977).

Support for I&Rs mounted as national reports endorsed their importance (Congressional Budget Office, 1978; Keniston & the Carnegie Council on Children, 1977) and as policy efforts took root in California and at the federal level. The initiatives experienced some success in California, but federal I&R policy initiatives were contained in the 1979 Child Care Act and became embroiled in its demise. Subsequent federal efforts, detailed in *CCI&R Issues* (October 1983; February 1984; July 1984; April 1985; September 1985; Spring 1986; Fall 1986) reveal both the tenacity of child care I&R advocates and their successes.

A historical turning point for the I&R movement, and one particularly germane to this analysis of collaboration, came with the publication of the *Project Connections* study (American Institutes for Research in the Behavioral Sciences, 1980). Funded jointly by the Day Care Division of the Administration for Children, Youth and Families (Office of Human Development Services, Department of Health, Education and Welfare) and the Ford Foundation, the study was designed to examine the cost and benefits of child-care information and referral services and to develop policy recommendations regarding alternative roles for the federal government with respect to I&R services. Because "no systematic study of these issues has previously been conducted, and virtually no base of information regarding the supply, distribution, effects and needs of child care information and referral services has been developed" (American Institutes for Research in the Behavioral Sciences, 1980, p. 1), the first phase of the study focused on generating a national profile of extant I&R services. Study authors divided the I&Rs into three categories: primary, major, or minor, with primaries characterized as autonomous units that defined their "*primary* mission as providing information and/or referral for child care on a regular basis" (p. 1, emphasis added). Morgan (1989) later noted: "When the study ended, it had become clear that these services were something quite different from an information service, and that the term 'resource and referral' would be a more appropriate term" (p. 1).

The vision of I&R had long incorporated a commitment to coordination, and the transition to the "resource and referral" (R&R) terminology made the commitment more explicit. The primaries were not simply providing information, but were engaged in important leadership efforts precipitating system reform: data collection across sites, joint training for providers, and advocacy work to remove regulatory barriers. While parents remained a significant audience for R&R work, critical services were also being rendered to providers, businesses (largely through contract work), and the community at large. Moreover, the potential for community leadership and organization became an integrated and visible mission for R&Rs. As documented by McConaghy and Siegel (1988), R&Rs "have the capability to address the three major policy dilemmas that challenge the child care delivery system: availability, quality, and affordability" (p. 3). But sadly, like so many other early care and education efforts, they faced the challenge of reconciling limited funding with unlimited expectation.

OTHER COLLABORATIVE EFFORTS OF THE 1970s

Early care and education collaborative efforts emerged in different settings and under different auspices during the 1970s. Although too numerous to document fully here, several of those most germane to creating linkages among early childhood service providers will be discussed.

Provider Service Networks

Less well known nationally, the Provider Service Network (PSN) project was launched in Santa Clara County, California, and represents a strategy that capitalizes on local planning and broad-based participation of early care and education specialists. Designed to integrate individuals and organizations into a network, PSNs, when they function optimally, provide organizational assistance, either helping par-

ticipating agencies function more effectively or creating new organizations to represent the interests of providers. Conceptually, there is
variability in what PSNs elect to do, but the range of options includes
launching demonstration and pilot programs, offering training and
technical assistance, conducting research and policy analysis, and
disseminating information. Less formal than other collaborative efforts, the PSN is an attempt to deal with the reality of interrelationships among individuals in the child-care community and to optimize
their interaction (Urban and Rural Systems Associates, 1977).

Day Care and the Schools

Different from the collaborations discussed thus far, the school–child-
care partnerships were designed primarily to provide direct services
for children and families, not to coordinate or consolidate the overall
child-care system. Nonetheless, important lessons for collaboration
emerge from a brief investigation of the day-care and schools efforts.

     While scholars, union officials, and education and child-care
leaders debated the appropriateness of linking child care and the
schools, practitioners forged ahead during the 1970s to establish effective partnerships. Their efforts took different forms, ranging from
providing infant and toddler care, preschool services, afterschool
care, family day care, or any of these in concert. Some of the programs
were *housed* in public schools and some not, some were *funded* by
public schools and some not, some were *staffed* with certified personnel and some not. Such diversity sheds light on a number of promising avenues for partnerships (Levine, 1978).

     Although programmatic diversity was extensive, the issues raised
were similar, transcending specific partnerships. Levine (1978) found
that although stable funding was often perceived as a benefit of co-
location in the schools, none of the programs in his sites realized
ongoing financial commitments from the schools. Endogenous eligibility and housing patterns did little to alter the basic income-
segregated system of early care and education. Personnel policies,
pay, and benefits remained sensitive areas in need of cross-system attention.

     Schools do offer a viable repository for programs and services,
but if systemic problems are not attended to, their involvement can
exacerbate an already inchoate delivery system. If these issues are
addressed, however, school involvement can be a powerful catalyst to
redress decades of fragmentation.

Head Start and the Schools

A leader in early care and education innovation in this nation, Head Start initiated several efforts to forge service and systemic links between its programs and the schools, including Head Start Planned Variation. But perhaps the most explicit embodiment of that goal was Project Developmental Continuity (PDC), designed to assure continuity of experience for children from Head Start through the early primary years and to develop models of continuity that could be implemented on a wide scale in nondemonstration communities (Office of Child Development, 1977). Though essentially a local program, PDC solicited input from the U.S. Office of Education, and state departments of education were involved in the site selection process. At a national level, the Education Commission of the States was engaged in a closely related effort that involved some of the states where the local PDC models were located. Results of the PDC effort indicated that Head Start/public school collaboration was a challenge in most of the communities, in spite of the additional resources provided by the project.

Undaunted, the Office of Child Development launched other efforts to link Head Start and the schools, including Basic Educational Skills and, in the 1980s, a transition project. Not unexpectedly, many of these efforts required the establishment of local councils to advise the projects. In some cases, they were broadly constructed and served as catalysts for change within a larger community (Chapel Hill Training Outreach Project, 1988). In retrospect, it can be seen that scholars and activists of the late 1960s and 1970s recognized the complexities of the problems and set out to rectify them with the best of intentions. Unfortunately, they were trapped in their own conceptual web; their solutions, like the system they were trying to save, were disorganized, idiosyncratic, and piecemeal. Too broad for such isolated responses, the challenge of collaboration was tacitly bequeathed to special education through legislation.

CHAPTER 7

The Special Case
of Special Education

THE FIELD OF SPECIAL EDUCATION provides a particularly fertile and
appropriate domain in which to study collaboration because (1) it is
inextricably tied to the delivery of services to young children and their
families, (2) it has experienced massive legislative attention, (3) it pays
particular importance to the role of families and multiple community
agencies, and (4) it has experience with, and a literature about, collaboration. This analysis, like that in preceding chapters, is not intended
to provide a comprehensive review of the many policy and programmatic issues associated with the history, legislation, and/or implementation of services to handicapped children. Rather, it is confined to an
analysis of collaboration within this domain.

HISTORY OF COLLABORATION IN SPECIAL EDUCATION

Reflecting the sociocultural changes recounted in Chapter 2, the field
of special education has been dramatically reformed during the past
decades. The civil rights movement and its aftermath led families with
handicapped children to reassess their rights. No longer content to
have their children isolated and receiving inferior services, parents of
the handicapped mobilized. With support from bureaucrats, politicians, and policy makers, a broad-scale effort manifested in legislation
took hold. For handicapped children, *least restrictive environment*,
mainstreaming, and *achieving maximum potential* were the by-words; for
parents, *due process* and *involvement*, suggesting greater collaboration,
were the goals.

In concert with this changed orientation toward equity and empowerment for children and their families, a new holistic view of
rehabilitation gained currency. Rather than requiring a single service
targeted to a particular need, handicapped children, like their nonhandicapped counterparts, were seen to have multiple needs, calling

for a more comprehensive approach to service delivery (Brewer & Kakalik, 1979; Katz & Martin, 1982; Paul, Stedman, & Neufeld, 1977).

Finally, recurrent charges of inhumane treatment and inadequate services for the handicapped captured public attention. With the atrocities of Willowbrook flashing across television screens and being pictorialized in books and news weeklies, there was little public doubt that services and the service system for the handicapped were in need of reform. A comprehensive analysis by the Rand Corporation in 1972 clearly confirmed this. After analyzing more than 50 state and federal programs, including those related to the U.S. Maternal and Child Health Services, Crippled Children's Services, and the Elementary and Secondary Education Act, the study concluded that all systems serving the needs of the handicapped were woefully inadequate, fragmented, uncoordinated, and in dire need of improvement (Brewer & Kakalik, 1979).

The mechanism for reform was the Education for All Handicapped Children Act of 1975 (P.L. 94-142), which mandated that free appropriate public education and related services were to be made available by 1980 to all handicapped children between the ages of 3 and 21. Excepted from coverage were children in the 0–3 and 18–21 age ranges in those states where school attendance laws did not include those ages. Of tremendous importance, P.L. 94-142 posed considerable challenges for the states and localities on many dimensions, including collaboration. Although the law did not require states to collaborate with other agencies per se, the tasks that were mandated—such as transportation, counseling, and diagnostic services—necessitated collaboration in order to comply with the law. With few resources and no explicit mandate, collaboration became the pot of gold at the end of the rainbow, the vision people sought, but with no concrete idea of how to attain it.

COLLABORATION IN P.L. 94-142

Fortunately, there is a good body of literature regarding the implementation of P.L. 94-142, with some of it directed toward understanding the role of collaboration in this process. Data have been collected from each of the 50 states in at least four studies, which are reviewed here, and many states have prepared their own comprehensive reports on interagency collaboration within their borders, four of which are included.

Initial reports on P.L. 94-142 were quite positive, indicating that it had a major impact on the delivery of direct services. However, the reports were more circumspect about the potential of the legislation to achieve system reform. Elder and Magrab (1980) claimed that it caused havoc in the system of service to the handicapped, but that it offered the potential to set things straight. Although they admitted the act potentially represented a revised federal role in funding and control, Brewer and Kakalik (1979) claimed that it was basically super-imposed on existing federal special education programs without fundamentally altering the system.

As we have seen, systemic reform is not easy to accomplish. However, P.L. 94-142 provides us with an excellent opportunity to better understand why this is so. The conceptual model suggested earlier in this book provides one window through which to view the events related to special education/early childhood collaboration. Our review underscores the important role mediating variables play as they affect normal developmental stages in shaping outcomes.

From a developmental perspective, the improvement of services to handicapped children began long before the passage of the legislation. Early stages took root as the press to improve services gained currency and legislation was considered. Well documented elsewhere, the legislative history of P.L. 94-142 took a good many turns and shifts, but once the law passed, attention turned to the complex implementation process. Unfortunately, an already complex process was made more so because the legislation mandated a dramatic shift in focus from federal to state and local levels. Required to maintain the final authority and responsibility for ensuring the provision of services to the handicapped, state education agencies (SEAs) found themselves suddenly front and center, bereft of the thinking and, in some cases, the commitment to what had heretofore been a more national effort. Certainly, if the states felt disenfranchised from the process, the local education agencies (LEAs), who were yet another step removed, were similarly ambivalent regarding their role in and commitment to the effort. From the beginning, state and local "buy-in" to the legislation was tentative, at best.

Such sentiment is not without cause or impact. Not only was the normal developmental sequence upset as the transition from federal to state and local levels was made, but critical variables were not shaped by those who were charged with implementation. The goals of the effort were nationally mandated, and although flexibility was accorded states, deviation in intent was not welcomed. In essence, conditions of mandate without the actual force of mandate were created, placing the effort in double jeopardy from the start. For these very reasons, theorists have questioned the effectiveness of mandate, suggesting that mandate can be a truly effective accelerator or simply an empty facade (Edgar & Maddox, 1983; Gray, 1985; Schopler, 1987; Warren, 1973).

The lack of clarity regarding mandate was not the only difficulty; the role of power and authority was severely miscalculated. Although charged with the responsibility to carry out the intent of the legislation, the SEAs and the LEAs did not control the services specified in the legislation, including diagnostic services, social work services, and physical and occupational therapy. Further, they did not have the resources, visibility, or authority that accrued to many of the agencies already serving the handicapped (Rogers & Farrow, 1983). They were stranded in the classic conundrum: they had responsibility without authority and, in this case, without sufficient resources. SEAs and LEAs were forced to build relationships with other, more powerful human service agencies to fulfill their charter (Elder & Magrab, 1980; Rogers & Farrow, 1983). Under these conditions, little egalitarian power sharing could be realized. The vital process of mutual adjustment and concession among the participants was inhibited (Warren, 1973).

Although difficulties in achieving real collaboration were accelerated by the structure imposed by the legislation, other elements in the context also inhibited attaining the desired results. Because of their historical autonomy, schools and local school districts were not "natural" collaborators. Professionalism, turf protection, and a captive market (via free schooling and compulsory attendance) are factors that have traditionally insulated schools from competing and/or linking with community services. As comparatively free-standing entities, SEAs and schools, when collaborating, have often remained reactive rather than proactive. Frequently, involvement occurred when other service agencies initiated efforts to accomplish their own objectives (Schenet, 1982). As a consequence, conventional models of school/community collaborations, where they existed, were based on inequality of status and participation (Rogers & Farrow, 1983).

Still other factors limited effective collaboration. Resource pooling (an essential component of collaboration, according to theorists) was complicated for several reasons. First, as indicated, the community agencies with budgets typically smaller than those of the schools already had the resources and responsibility for some of the mandated tasks. What did they have to gain from the pooling of resources? Second, slightly akin to Pandora's box and clearly reminiscent of the history of mainstream early care and education, the costs associated with this legislation, though difficult to estimate, were going to be high. From the early stages, critics doubted the ability to fund the hoped-for reforms (Brewer & Kakalik, 1979). Without assurance of federal support, there was little incentive for current service providers to take on more responsibility. With the advent of the Reagan administration, the devolution of even greater responsibility to the states, state shortfalls, and a 20% reduction in outlays for human services between 1980 and 1988 (*U.S. Budget in Brief*, 1989), uncertainties escalated.

But it was not solely the amount of resources available that raised concern. In cases where funds were adequate, limitations imposed by the funding sources often prevented the flexible use of money for interagency efforts (Rogers & Farrow, 1983). Together, lack of resources and limitations in their distribution delayed collaborative activity in P.L. 94-142.

While constraints on finances were stringent, there was some flexibility in other provisions that has been alternately praised and criticized. The passage of the law was unaccompanied by strict federal guidelines governing activity at the state or local levels. As a consequence, states have tailored their collaborative structures, their participants, and their activities to meet the needs and demands of their locales. This flexibility of configuration led researchers to find that successful collaboration is most often locally arranged (Fletcher & Cole, 1988; Schenet, 1982), supporting the theory that participative decision making is essential to collaboration. But despite local-level satisfaction with the freedom associated with flexibility, some authors criticize the results. The lack of guidelines was accompanied by inadequate training by the federal government, exacerbating the lack of qualified personnel. Further, critics point to the lack of a uniform approach to problem solving, which resulted in disparities in standards of educational quality (Rogers & Farrow, 1983).

In sum, after more than a decade of attempted collaborative activity in special education, researchers conclude that there is great variation in the actual collaborations in action, but that there is very little coordination among programs (Allington & Johnston, 1989; Edgar & Maddox, 1983; Helge, 1984; Johnson et al., 1982; Katz & Martin, 1982; Morgan, 1985; Rogers & Farrow, 1983; Schenet, 1982). At the heart of these limited successes is the failure to integrate two essential defining characteristics of collaboration espoused by theorists: sharing of authority and pooling of resources.

Despite the failure of most states to achieve egalitarian power sharing or pooling of resources and the uncertainty surrounding the success of collaborative efforts, researchers found a number of very positive outcomes. For example, SEAs that were able to resolve turf battles and moderate the impact of resource uncertainty engaged in four common activities, all of which were related to collaborative leadership. Using interagency agreements as the vehicle, successful SEAs (1) clarified agency responsibilities for handicapped students in state-operated residential programs; (2) promoted local interagency collaboration, using agreements or financial incentives; (3) established general state policy with regard to service delivery and financial responsibilities among agencies, facilitating agreements among local agencies; and (4) aided information sharing among agencies. SEAs were also judged most effective when they promoted interagency collaborations (Rogers & Farrow, 1983; Schenet, 1982).

Certainly formal agreements at the state level do not always promote similar agreements or productive collaborations at the local level (Schenet, 1982). Yet along with common goals and resource sharing, individual state analyses suggest that agreements can accelerate collaborative activity. In unpublished reports (Jones & Stegelin, 1988), Kentucky and Ohio indicate that agencies identify common goals and sharing of resources as among the critical factors in collaboration. Confirming the importance of common goals, the Maryland analysis suggests that they should not only be mutually acceptable but also precisely defined (Maryland State Department of Education, 1983).

How states allocate power and authority is sometimes omitted from state discussions of collaboration. For example, neither the Kentucky nor the Ohio report suggested how participants handle issues of power and authority among themselves, although the Ohio study indicates that the matter of turf can be a major factor inhibiting collaboration. Where discussed, building trust, sharing power, and even rotating leadership are considered important components of successful collaboration.

COLLABORATION AMONG RURAL SPECIAL EDUCATION EFFORTS

Nowhere is the study of collaboration more interesting than in rural settings. Often omitted from discussion, the rural experience, particularly with respect to 94-142, is especially instructive. If absence of resources is a motivating force for collaborative activity, then rural America should be at the forefront of these efforts, certainly with respect to P.L. 94-142. Because federal funding prohibited the direct passing of funds from states to localities with too few eligible children, small rural districts were encouraged to form collaborations.

Researchers expected that rural special education collaboration would be motivated primarily by federal funding criteria. In fact, a 1980 survey conducted by the National Rural Research Project and reported by Helge (1984) revealed that the vast majority (73%) of rural special education providers reported a desire to enhance service delivery as their primary incentive to collaborate with others. Confirmed by Fletcher and Cole (1988), this finding suggests that the propensity to collaborate is a strong motivation, regardless of resources, in rural areas. Such commitment may be accelerated by mandate, in that 72% of the states legislate or regulate systems of collaboration among rural special education efforts (Fletcher & Cole, 1988).

Given that collaboration is so prevalent in rural areas, it would be helpful to look at these programs to discern the variables or structures that seem to correlate with collaborative effectiveness. Yet the literature suggests that no one specific type of arrangement is considered most effective (Fletcher & Cole, 1988; Helge, 1984). Such variation has been considered the key to collaborative success in that a majority of respondents were greatly satisfied with their current system (Fletcher & Cole, 1988). Alternately, as is the case with nonrural collaborations, such flexibility fuels concerns over the variability and inconsistency of roles and definitions (Edgar & Maddox, 1983; Johnson et al., 1982). Authors suggest that this flexibility obfuscates who is responsible for what and prevents the generalizability of experience from one locale to another.

COLLABORATION IN P.L. 99-457

Those close to special education and educational reform suggest that P.L. 94-142, though it fell short of its many goals, made a significant impact on the delivery of services to handicapped children. In an effort to address shortfalls in the original legislation and to expand those covered by federal legislation, the Education of the Handicapped Act amendments of 1986 (P.L. 99-457, Part H) were enacted. Unlike its predecessor, P.L. 99-457 included provisions for serving handicapped children from birth to age 3 and expanded parental provisions (Garwood, Fewell, & Neisworth, 1988; Trohanis, 1989). In addition, the act aims to achieve systemic reform, requiring that states transform their fragmented delivery systems into a comprehensive, multidisciplinary, coordinated one (Gallagher, Harbin, Thomas, Clifford, & Wenger, 1988). Harbin and McNulty (1990) point out that P.L. 99-457 contains several mechanisms that ensure the development and implementation of a coordinated system of services. For example, a primary vehicle for achieving collaboration is the mandated Interagency Coordinating Council (ICC) appointed by the governor to ensure the development and implementation of a statewide system of services that is coordinated across public and private agencies. This mechanism is reinforced by the designation of a lead agency that coordinates with other agencies in planning and administering the program. Finally, at the local level, mandated individual family service plans (IFSPs) are designed to foster cross-agency and cross-disciplinary planning to meet family needs. Such an enmeshed and pervasive commitment to collaboration has led some observers to infer that legislators recognized the limited success of P.L. 94-142 and plunged into full-scale reform of the infrastructure in lieu of merely providing more resources to current programs (Gallagher et al., 1988).

Whatever the motivation, it is clear that the collaborative provisions were necessary. At the inception of P.L. 99-457, state administration and provision of services were found to be divided among multiple agencies, with typically three to four responsible for managing early intervention services: as might be expected, diverse funding patterns accompanied diverse administrative arrangements (Meisels, Harbin, Modigliani, & Olson, 1988). To stem these difficulties, states were asked to identify those services in the greatest need of collaboration (case management, staff training, diagnostic assessment, and intervention programs) and those barriers that most inhibited collaboration (lack of funds, limitation on use of funds, inconsistent eligibility criteria, lack of interagency coordination, and inconsistent regulations across agencies) (Meisels et al., 1988). Compounding the problem, interagency members often lack experience in interagency work, negotiation skills, conflict resolution skills, and vision and leadership to see beyond current structural solutions (Harbin & McNulty, 1990). Moreover, prior to P.L. 99-457, federally funded state programs (Medicaid, Early and Periodic Screening, Diagnosis, and Treatment Program [EPSDT], Developmental Disabilities Block Grant programs, Maternal and Child Health, and Title XX Social Service programs) had "never been required to share *fiscal and programmatic* responsibility for a single program, as they [were] required to do under Part H" (Pontzer, 1989, p. 4; emphasis added).

P.L. 99-457 provides both the opportunity and the responsibility to foster collaboration not simply within special education but across disciplines, governmental levels, and economic sectors, not to mention the important avenue generated for solidifying links between providers of services to handicapped and nonhandicapped children. In the process, states and localities are faced with resolving some of the most difficult challenges associated with collaboration: setting goals, sharing power and resources, discerning and using flexibility, defining parameters (in this case, something as basic as "developmentally disabled"), and establishing structures to deal with the tasks ahead (Harbin, Terry, & Daguio, 1989).

Given the complexity of the issues and the freshness of the task, there is only limited information presently available on how collaborative efforts in P.L. 99-457 are faring. Fortunately, talented groups are tracking the process, so rich information should be forthcoming fairly regularly. We do know that the primary collaborative vehicles at the state level, the ICCs, are in various stages of implementation. Conducted under the auspices of the Mental Health Law Project, one study examined the implementation of the ICCs and found that their experiences were quite different in the 11 states studied (Pontzer, 1989). Formal decision-making structures were evident in only a few of the states. Some had established high-level interagency planning groups separate from their ICCs, a process condoned by parents and advocates. Although not as robust as had been anticipated, ICC proactive roles were escalating. Implementation delays were attributed not to the inefficacy of the ICC structure, but to more pervasive problems regarding the public's awareness of P.L. 99-457, the involvement of sufficiently representative participants, and the need for more deft state-local articulation.

In addition to the concerns listed above, others have suggested that the lack of coordination at the federal level is a major barrier to collaboration—a theme reminiscent of the early care and education literature. Harbin and McNulty (1990) suggest that federal agencies have done little to examine their own policies regarding collaboration; rather, they have given responsibility to the states without acknowledging that their own limited involvement may be a significant hindrance. "Unless the federal agencies are willing to tackle the problems of service eligibility, funding, and certification, the promise of service coordination may never come to fruition" (Harbin & McNulty, 1990, pp. 48–49).

Without doubt, practitioners, policy makers, advocates, and parents concerned about the implementation of P.L. 99-457 will have much to teach the field about collaboration. On the other hand, if early findings are indicative, we will all have much to learn. P.L. 99-457 has the potential to be a guiding light to collaborators as they grapple with the complex issues inherent in today's unique social, political, and ideological context.

CHAPTER 8

The Labyrinth of Current Collaborative Efforts

"It must be understood that federal participation in education, health and social service programs does not follow any grand design."

Jule M. Sugarman, 1989

THE GOAL OF THIS CHAPTER is to discuss today's enthusiasm for collaboration and place it in realistic perspective. Is collaboration a 1990s fad, an empty platitude, a naive expectation? Or is there something significantly different about today's context and today's efforts that will infuse collaboration with enduring vitality? Is the context sufficiently strong, the systemic pain sufficiently deep, to support a construct that has had such an ephemeral history?

COLLABORATION IN THE 1990s CONTEXT

Factors Precipitating a New *Zeitgeist*

There are over 11 million children aged 3 to 5 in the United States today. For most, growing up will be a dramatically different experience than it was for children just a decade ago (National Academy of Sciences, 1990). Many more youngsters will be only children; will have working, teenaged, and/or single parents; will live away from their extended families; will move frequently in their young lives; and will grow up in poverty. New family patterns, along with changes in women's workforce participation and the reescalation of poverty, have escaped few Americans' attention. This is the 1990s American Rorschach, an image simultaneously suggesting massive social reorganization and increased social need.

It is probable that this internal social revolution would have prompted some political response, even if it were a stand-alone phenomenon. But it is not. Internal changes are paralleled by massive external realignments of power and commerce. America's longstanding hegemony is being challenged as globalization takes root. No longer the economic center of the world, the United States has seen its business and industrial prominence eclipsed. Compelling social changes coupled with equally compelling productivity needs yield sound economic motivation for maximizing America's human capital.

Such legitimate concern about the future workforce has propelled corporate America to take careful stock of our nation's workforce preparation. In so doing, it has rendered support to education in unprecedented amounts and forms (National Alliance of Business, 1989, 1990). Large corporations are making significant financial commitments to the care and education of young children through contributions to resource and referral efforts, direct support to parents, and major national initiatives to improve the quality of care. Respected businesspeople prod Congress to allocate significant increases to Head Start's budget. Reporting cost data unavailable even a decade ago, American business leaders have recognized the effectiveness and cost-effectiveness of early intervention. Business support has been a significant factor in creating an entirely new climate for early care and education.

A second factor encouraging collaboration, precipitated in part by the first, has been the increased willingness of elected officials to become involved in early care and education issues. At the highest level, the president has advocated the largest single increase in Head Start's budget since the inception of the program 25 years ago. And national goals now begin with a commitment to "ready" all young children for school. In Congress, representatives from both sides of the aisle, although they may not be in full accord on strategies, recognize and support the need for more child-care services. In contrast, even just a few years ago, conservative lawmakers disputed the need for such legislation.

Changes are manifest at the state level as well. Some of the most significant leadership efforts have been exerted in statehouses and state legislatures, resulting in substantially increased services and in repeated pleas for coordination. Indeed, even by 1989, the number of states making contributions to early childhood programs had risen to 31, nearly quadrupling the number in the prior decade (Mitchell, 1989).

A third factor accounting for a changing *Zeitgeist* relates to the accumulation of our collective knowledge. Widely popularized research bespeaks the effectiveness and cost-effectiveness of early intervention for low-income children, leaving little doubt of its personal and social value (Berrueta-Clement, Schweinhart, Barnett, Epstein, & Weikart, 1984; Lazar & Darlington, 1982). Moreover, in response to ideas of leaders in the field (Caldwell, 1986), distinctions between care and education are toppling. With the publication of *Developmentally Appropriate Practice* (Bredekamp, 1987), the field has codified quality elements that transcend individual early education settings. In the new ethos, what distinguishes programs is quality, not idiosyncratic labels affixed to doorways.

In addition to increasing our knowledge about quality, we have increased our understanding of how to construct and implement successful programs. Schorr's work (1988) suggests that successful programs are comprehensive, flexible, and responsive; they deal with the child within the context of family and community; they provide staff with the time, training, skills, and institutional resources to create secure environments; and they are well managed, usually by highly competent, energetic individuals. Elaborating on the attributes of managers of effective programs, Golden (1988, 1989) suggests that willingness to take risks, tolerate ambiguity, win trust, and recruit and supervise staff collaboratively are important, but not necessarily magical, qualities.

Perhaps as a result of the above factors, a fourth factor—changing values—also contours the collaborative context. Without doubt, subtle stigmas that accompanied out-of-home care for children, particularly between ages 3 and 5, have dissipated. The shroud of the "domestic ethic" that obscured the real need for child care and education is all but gone, as mothers flock to the paid workforce. And as the stigma has been lifted and early care and education legitimized as a societal imperative, the call for collaboration sounds.

In addition to altering our values, new knowledge has also modified how we frame the problem—a fifth contextual factor. Heretofore, rationales for poor services were often based on dilemmas of individual programs or administrators. Through mounting data, we came to realize that while these variables certainly constituted part of the problem, they were not the sole cause. We saw that even with good programs and good administrators, services still languished. Such realizations forced practitioners and policy makers to move beyond program-level thinking and to recognize that service dilemmas are nested in and inextricably influenced by systemic problems.

The popular will to alter widely accepted systemic dysfunctions in human services constitutes another significant contextual factor. Those concerned about collaboration in early care and education are not alone; the problems that characterize their service delivery are broadly manifest. Melaville and Blank (1991), in reflecting on how we

have failed our children, synthesize reasons that the system is ineffective in meeting current needs: the system divides the problems of
children and families into distinct categories that inhibit interrelated
solutions; communication across system components is dysfunctional; and training and funding are insufficient and inefficient.

To alleviate schisms in service delivery, a broad commitment to
collaboration has taken root, augmenting the knowledge and strategies available to those particularly concerned about young children
and their families. Links among human service, health, and education departments are burgeoning on the federal, state, and local levels. Organizations from the public and private sectors are promoting
collaboration, with notable leadership being provided by national
foundations, for example, the Annie E. Casey Foundation's New Futures effort. The National Governors' Association "encourages states
to integrate their services and create a comprehensive, client-focused
network. . . . State regulations that impede collaboration at the state
and local level should be eliminated" (National Governors' Association, 1990, p. 21). Moreover, 20 national organizations concerned with
interagency efforts to connect children and families with comprehensive services have banded together to form the Education and Human
Services Consortium.

A New *Zeitgeist*

In the early 1990s, it appears that support for collaboration runs deep
and is somewhat different from past efforts. Clearly, support is broader and is characterized by many new constituents—businesspeople,
politicians, parents, and media. Further, 1990s collaboration was not
invented by Washington bureaucrats so that it could be excised from
policy as quickly as it was initiated. Rather, it has emerged from the
real needs of families and children in municipalities across the nation.
And perhaps most important, the majority of today's supporters of
collaboration are fiercely realistic. They do not regard collaboration as
a panacea. They know it is a means to an end, not an end in itself
(Bruner, 1991). And they know that effective collaboration is difficult
to achieve.

Within early care and education, this new *Zeitgeist* is particularly
unique and distinguished from past efforts. In addition to the reasons
above that pertain to current collaborative efforts across the human
services, 1990s early care and education collaboratives are particularly
robust for two reasons. First, the field is experiencing expansion at
unprecedented rates. This expansion has given rise to a rethinking of
service delivery strategies in the field. Some advance tax credits, oth-

ers advance direct support to providers; some want human service–based programs, others want new initiatives housed in education, and still others want states and municipalities to make such decisions; some policies are driven by a welfare orientation, others are driven by a special education orientation. Indeed, the plethora of support for early care and education is matched by an equal plethora of ideas about how best to meet the needs. While this is an intellectually fertile period, there is little agreement and less data on which strategies are most effective. In the absence of such agreement, practitioners and policy makers are turning to collaboration as one potential strategy. Rapid growth and a lack of consensus fuel collaboration.

Second, 1990s early care and education collaboration is different from past efforts because there is growing recognition that the already frail infrastructure simply cannot support all the new initiatives in the field. As programs mushroom, the infrastructure weakens in various ways. The supply of providers is already inadequate. And because the field lacks sufficient salary or status incentives, the quality of those entering it will be diminished even more. Training is poorly coordinated and ill fashioned to meet the field's burgeoning demands (Rockefeller Brothers Foundation, 1990). Providers compete for scarce resources—space and staff (Goodman & Brady, 1988)—and personnel turnover increases as workers pursue better salaries and opportunities (Whitebook, Howes, & Phillips, 1989). With only limited provisions for integrating low-income children or for meeting the needs of full-time working parents in all the programs, the patchwork service quilt grows larger, but not stronger. Concerns about diminishing equity and access flourish (Kagan, 1989; Mitchell et al., 1989; Scarr & Weinberg, 1986). Consequently, there is recognition that this is a critical juncture for early care and education. Not only does program expansion provide an opportunity to craft a more comprehensive and integrated system, but there is a sense that not doing so will fell the system. If ever there was a time for collaboration in early care and education, this is it.

1990s COLLABORATIONS AT THE FEDERAL, STATE, AND LOCAL LEVELS

How do these calls for collaboration actually manifest themselves in the real world? Is this simply a rhetorical movement, limited to esoteric discussion? What evidence do we have that collaboration is actually taking root?

As the following discussion suggests, collaboration is taking hold throughout the nation. Collaborations dot the federal landscape in executive and legislative domains. They operate in nearly every state and in many municipalities. They have linked profit and nonprofit sectors in communities throughout the nation. Nearly ubiquitous, collaborative efforts are difficult to chronicle in their entirety. Consequently, the discussion below, and the program descriptions that constitute the Appendix, should be regarded as examples of a very broad array of efforts. Representative in diversity and flavor, they convey the sense of the collaborative *Zeitgeist* in early care and education.

Federal Legislative Initiatives

Support for collaboration is manifest in several major pieces of legislation. As discussed earlier, P.L. 99-457 is the most robust legislation favoring collaboration. With its funding and explicit mandate requiring interagency councils, many regard it as the legislative trendsetter in forging links among agencies to render improved services for children and families.

Not alone in collaborative intent, P.L. 99-457 is joined by the Family Support Act (FSA), the nation's welfare reform legislation passed in 1988. FSA provides for the inclusion of existing early childhood education programs, including Head Start, Chapter I, and school and nonprofit programs in planning the implementation of its child-care provisions. It requires that Aid to Families with Dependent Children child care be coordinated with these programs and encourages states to undertake comprehensive studies of supply and need. Given that the FSA is likely to generate dramatic increases in the need for child care, such commitments to collaborative planning and service delivery are essential. Moreover, many of the children needing care through this act will have significant developmental needs, potentially requiring the combined attention of multiple service providers in a given community. Still in its infancy, the FSA is likely to be an important catalyst for collaboration at state and local levels.

The Augustus F. Hawkins Human Services Reauthorization Act of 1990 provides for collaboration in several different ways. To forge stronger links between Head Start and the schools, the act includes a new Head Start Transition Project that encourages collaborations among Head Start, the schools, and providers of other services. Each project must have a plan to coordinate family outreach and support efforts, and provision is made for the establishment of consortia to meet this goal. Closer links with Follow Through are also fostered in the act. Moreover, a separate Title (IX) of the act, Coordinated Services for Children, Youth and Families, calls for the establishment of a Federal Council on Children, Youth and Families. Independent state bodies would be established to determine mechanisms for the distribution of new dollars for service programs. Such provisions clearly underscore the need for more comprehensive services and the need for better planning and cross-agency collaboration.

The Child Care and Development Block Grant of 1991 (also known as the Act for Better Child Care) traveled a long and arduous path. Early drafts had provisions for collaboration in both the Senate and the House versions. On the Senate side, there was a provision for the establishment of state interagency advisory committees with local advisory councils. On the House side, while there were no provisions for state advisory committees, the bill called for local advisory councils that would be broadly representative of the community. In a very complex set of negotiations, these provisions were deleted from the final act. Some felt they would have added another layer of bureaucracy; others wanted dollars to go into direct services for children. While the legislation encourages collaborations among providers, it does little to actively establish the vehicles by which such collaborations might take place.

Despite the elimination of direct funding for collaborations, the process of enacting this legislation was helpful to the collaborative enterprise on several counts. Perhaps most significantly, it established a forum where many, though not all, representatives of the child-care and early education industry came together. Under the leadership of the Children's Defense Fund, more than 139 organizations have come together at the national level to form the Alliance for Better Child Care, an impressive group that works to enhance the development and implementation of legislation to foster a comprehensive, collaborative delivery system. Moreover, the group was instrumental in establishing collaborative policy entities in many states, an important structural legacy.

By negotiating the inclusion of collaborative mechanisms in early drafts of the legislation, the early care and education community not only informed legislators and legislative staff of the importance of collaboration but also set the stage for more holistic thinking about child care and early education. Through testimony and extensive discussion, systemic problems of inequity, fragmentation, and access were emphasized. Leaders in the field and in the executive branch better understood that new thinking was necessary. No longer could the field tolerate program approaches to systemic problems. Mandated or not, the need for collaboration became clear.

Federal Executive Initiatives

Beyond legislative initiatives, support for collaboration among the Departments of Education, Health and Human Services, and Labor is building. Cooperative planning on several major national studies is underway, and several joint meetings regarding future research initiatives have been held. For example, the Department of Education has funded a national study of joint transition efforts by Head Start and the schools and, with support from the Department of Health and Human Services, is stimulating work on transitions within the Office of Educational Research and Improvement (OERI) Centers. Moreover, these departments have formed a joint Head Start/Compensatory Education Task Force with the explicit goals of (1) strengthening the transition from Head Start to school; (2) sustaining gains made by Head Start and other preschool programs during the early years in school; and (3) fostering coordination of Head Start with compensatory education programs, especially the Chapter 1 and Even Start programs (J. MacDonald, personal communication, July 1990).

Efforts to promote collaboration among Head Start and other agencies serving young children, while always strong, have been given an added boost by the funding of 12 demonstration programs especially designed to foster collaboration at the state level. Additionally, Head Start grantees and school systems throughout America are being encouraged to form links with child-care and early education providers (Administration for Children, Youth and Families, 1990; Maximus, Inc., 1988). Moreover, the Administration for Children, Youth and Families has entered into a close relationship with the Family Support Administration to foster collaboration between Head Start and the JOBS program.

State and Local Initiatives

Many collaborative initiatives are taking root in the states, sometimes under the aegis of federal programs. In addition to P.L. 99-457 efforts, P.L. 100-77 (the Stewart B. McKinney Homeless Assistance Act), the Maternal and Child Health Block Grant and its programs for children with special health needs, and the National Institute of Mental Health's Child and Adolescent Service Program require states to develop interagency councils and to coordinate planning and service delivery as a condition for federal funding. Even in states where a penchant for collaboration predated the legislation, the mandate has accelerated it. In other states, legislatures or governors have launched special commissions or task forces to address specific problems. In some, the ethos for collaboration is so strong that it permeates the majority of new initiatives (e.g., Florida), while in others it may be an isolated group working on a specific problem.

Whatever the impetus for collaboration, the actual efforts are carried out through a myriad of structures. Collaborative councils established by governors, either as a result of or independent of mandate, have increased collaboration in some states. The work of legislatively based committees, interagency councils, or governors' human services cabinets has also increased collaboration (e.g., Texas and Connecticut). In some states, offices to promulgate and coordinate child care have been established (e.g., Pennsylvania, Virginia, and Washington, D.C.) or state child-care policy coordinators have been hired (e.g., Rhode Island). Some states have established special demonstration programs with a focus on collaboration (e.g., New Jersey's Urban PreKindergarten Program). And National Association for the Education of Young Children (NAEYC) affiliates have been active in accelerating collaboration elsewhere.

THE MANY FACES OF 1990s COLLABORATION

In trying to better understand collaborative structure, it has been suggested that collaborations often take one of four forms: interagency councils, advisory councils, offices of child care, or interagency agreements (Mitchell et al., 1989). Bruner (1991), in his work on state-level collaboration, offers a helpful hierarchy. He suggests that first-generation approaches are those initiated from the top down, usually through the establishment of interagency task forces or commissions. In this phase, state policy makers direct agencies to plan together to address child and family needs. Second-generation approaches support collaborative initiatives, often in the form of demonstration projects that are accompanied by some finances and technical assistance. Typically sites are selected for their ability to develop replicable models. Bruner's third-generation approaches are more pervasive and seek comprehensive, statewide collaboration among multiple agencies. They may also involve mechanisms to develop leadership that will support successful programs. Examples of all three approaches may be found in the program descriptions in the Appendix.

Finally, Kagan, Rivera, and Lamb-Parker (1990) suggest that collaborations may be classified along multiple dimensions, including their impetus (mandate or voluntary), their locale (state, local, or both), and their mission (system, service, or both). This framework is helpful when discussing collaborations not only at the state level but also at the local level, where they seem to be particularly plentiful.

Different from their state counterparts, local collaborations are often *voluntarily* initiated to stave off impending crises in service delivery. For example, disquieted by the lack of afterschool care, some work to increase these services. Some establish services to assist parents through public information campaigns or pamphlet distributions; others assist programs by creating employment directories or establishing substitute teacher registries. Some local collaborations have been short-lived, but increasingly many have become more permanent because they have been particularly successful in obtaining corporate or foundation dollars to execute specific projects or services. Building from the crisis orientation and fueled by their successes, many local collaborations adopt new activities and turn their energies to system or service delivery issues, for example, by assuring comparability of entry regulations for children and standards for programs or by working for pay comparability across systems. These local collaborations are particularly successful in triggering community interest and support (Euben & Reisman, 1990). Without the force or requirements of mandate, they also can be quite flexible and responsive. Some collaborations initiated by concerns for young children have broadened their agenda, while others remain resolutely committed to younger populations.

This is not to suggest that all local collaborations are voluntary in nature or that local collaborations are easier to implement than state efforts. Exciting collaborations have emerged at the local level as a result of mandate. Sometimes the mandate takes the form of a mayoral or city council decree; sometimes it is the local component of a state or federal initiative. Typically, locally mandated collaborations are themselves direct policy-making entities or advisory bodies to such entities. In either case, they acquire clout because they are composed of key governmental and, sometimes, key business, players. As such, they can be powerful forces for change within the public sector. Paradoxically, although they are usually responsible for long-range planning, long-term databases, or determining future program directions, their primary problem is durability: the sacred cow of one political administration, they may well become the sacrificial lamb of the next.

An additional and promising type of collaboration is emerging in some states. Dubbed "vertical collaboration," it is the combination of state and local efforts. In these cases a state council may garner legislative support and funding for a series of local collaborative efforts. The local entities are the implementation arms of the combined effort and are linked to one another and to the state collaboration, sharing experiences and shaping policy. Confirming recent literature (Fuhrman & Elmore, 1990), this approach fosters synergy between state and local efforts. Contrary to the often perceived unidirectional flow of control from state to local organizations, each level strongly influences and informs the other. Examples of this approach exist in Virginia and Oregon and are being considered elsewhere.

Although few in number, these examples of collaborations at work provide a glimpse into the diversity of effort, structure, and mission. Beyond pointing to their diversity, the intent in discussing current collaborative efforts is to convey the richness of today's collaborative *Zeitgeist*. It *is* different from decades past, when directives were externally imposed or when funding was the raison d'être. Today, many collaborations are homegrown, tailored to particular needs and enjoy strong public support. They seem to be an integral part of their communities and meaningful to their participants.

Aside from being more numerous, today's collaborations are different in that they are truly collaborative. As the state-local examples suggest, commitment to sharing, to achieving mutual goals, and to recognizing individual or institutional talents makes these efforts collaborative in their very process. Different in intent and in process from the past, 1990s collaborations promise to become a prominent feature in the early childhood landscape, filling present needs while striving to meet those of the future. And in their very bounty, they provide spiritual hope and practical lessons.

CHAPTER 9

Sacred Cows and Sacrificial Lambs: Lessons from Recent Collaborations

"Real progress . . . is possible only when communities move beyond cooperation to genuinely collaborative ventures at both the service delivery and system level."

Melaville and Blank, 1991

THERE IS AMPLE EVIDENCE that collaboration in early care and education is taking root. The critical question to which we now turn is: What difference does it make? How do we know when we have achieved success? What have we really learned from these pioneering efforts? Though data continue to be amassed, we have mounting literature that demonstrates the challenges of evaluating collaborations. And we have a growing body of studies that shed light on the processes and outcomes of collaboration. This chapter suggests that while the state of the art of evaluating collaborations is somewhat embryonic, much work is emerging to suggest that collaborations are effective catalysts for change and that there is much to be learned from their processes.

CHALLENGES OF EVALUATING SUCCESSFUL COLLABORATIONS

How do we know when collaborations are successful? Although apparently simple, the question is deceptively complex. In part, it is complex because so many of today's collaborations are comparatively new, with energy being appropriately devoted to implementation. Few collaborations chronicle their accomplishments in any systematic way, and fewer outside evaluators or academics who normally study social phenomena have been drawn to the issue.

But even for those who do chronicle and evaluate collaborative processes and outcomes, significant challenges exist. To assess the efficacy of collaborative efforts, at least three conditions must be met. First, the goals of the endeavor must be explicitly clear. Second, in order to evaluate the collaboration it must be implemented; and third, the standards of measurement must be precise and replicable. Using these criteria, the evaluation of collaborative efforts poses several challenges.

First, there is the challenge of defining the goal. Most agree—and literature and practice confirm—that collaboration is a means to an end, not an end in itself. Therefore, there is a justifiable desire to evaluate the efficacy of collaborations by their ends. Stressing accountability, policy makers want to know how collaboration has changed child or family outcome. What performance indices have been altered as a result of the collaboration? At the heart of the issue is the question of how do we define collaborative success: How do we know when we have hit a home run?

A growing number of those who investigate collaborations are suggesting that collaborations have two broad goals: producing direct *services* and fostering or creating *system* change (Kagan et al., 1990; Melaville & Blank, 1991), with some collaborations attempting both. Despite mounting consensus on these broad goals, debate persists on whether collaborations should be held accountable for changes in child and family outcome (Bruner, 1991) or changes in service delivery and system reform. Advocates of using child and family outcomes as indices of success suggest that collaborations' ultimate utility is to improve life conditions for children and families. If so, then why not hold them accountable for these ends? Those who favor changes in delivery as the index of success say that collaborations should not be held accountable for ends when their focus is on changing the means. Moreover, they correctly suggest that many interventions may combine to alter child and family outcome; such changes cannot be directly or solely attributed to collaborative impact.

Closer examination reveals that the ends-means dilemma is only part of the problem of defining success. Two additional dimensions of collaboration complicate the success definition. First, because of their inherent complexity, collaborations have multiple process and outcome dimensions, complicating the challenge of defining precise success criteria. Does success mean accomplishing all, half, a third? Or does success mean being partially successful on all dimensions or fully successful on a few? Moreover, because the context for collaboration varies so, what might be regarded as an accomplishment in one setting may be taken for granted in another. Golden, Skinner, and Baker (1990), in underscoring the difficulties of determining success and in affirming the importance of context, suggest that we might do well to rely on "program elements that are operationally effective in their circumstances" (p. 29). Rather than seeking overall indices of success or dubbing efforts as exemplary models, we may do well to consider partial conditions of success within specific circumstances.

The second factor, the degree of implementation, remains equally problematic. If one is going to attribute outcome to an intervention, one must be certain that the intervention has been implemented. But since collaborations are designed to be flexible and meet changing needs, their implementation is never complete. No precise definition of implementation exists because it is a highly idiosyncratic and mutable condition. Indeed, the strength of collaborations is that they are tailored to meet changing local circumstances. For example, it is not uncommon to find collaborations that deem themselves well implemented one day and fledgling the next. Such changes are predictable and underscore the evaluation dilemma; while implementation flux is a practical necessity, it remains an empirical nightmare.

Less problematic than and less influenced by the above challenges, agreed-upon evaluation methodology remains distant. It is clear that, unlike quantitative studies that examine limited interventions, collaboration is amenable to qualitative investigation. And although solid advances have been made in case study methodology (Yin, 1989), appropriate evaluation methods suitable to the precise needs of collaborative enterprises are still being debated.

COLLABORATIONS CAN AND DO WORK

Despite these very real limitations, the picture is not so grim. Through case study and other qualitative methods, evidence that collaborations are making a difference is mounting. From interviews with individuals involved in collaborative work come consistent responses that they feel successful. Often expressing their success in terms of enhanced trust, communication, and understanding, collaborators hasten to report that simply bringing together diverse groups who have never spoken, thereby establishing the collaboration, is an important accomplishment. And indeed it is.

Examples of successful collaborations dot national reports, including *Joining Forces* (Levy & Copple, 1989), *Right from the Start* (National Association of State Boards of Education, 1989), and *What It Takes* (Melaville & Blank, 1991). These reports suggest that collaborations take many different forms and that success means something quite different for each. For example, California's New Beginnings, begun in 1988, has both service delivery initiatives and systemic change as intended outcomes. The Ventura County Mental Health Department's Children's Demonstration Project aims to coordinate extant services and to use resources differently. The goal of the Savannah, Georgia, New Futures Initiative Project is "to trigger and sustain a political process that is powerful enough not only to modify established institutions, but actually to redefine their objectives, their accountability and their interrelationships" (Joe & Nelson, 1989, p. 221).

Within the early care and education field, stunning examples of accomplishing collaborations exist (Kagan et al., 1990). To obtain their information, the researchers selected 72 collaborations from a stratified random sample of 300 and conducted in-depth telephone interviews with a representative from each. Despite the obvious limitations of a single-contact, self-report telephone survey, the results depict an interesting panorama of what collaborations are accomplishing.

Most representatives indicated that the collaborations were making improvements in quality, either through training, continuity of services provided, or enhanced parent involvement. Seventy-four percent of the collaborations studied had expanded training options for teachers in programs, 69% had increased joint planning and communication among caregivers in their communities, and 76% had launched explicit efforts to help parents feel a stronger bond with their programs. Comprehensiveness of services, a commonly recognized goal, was achieved by 78% of the collaborations in the study.

Collaborations were also active in more systemic issues. To facilitate access to services, 90% of the studied collaborations had helped parents by accessing information; others had supported parents as they formed advocacy networks. Over half the collaborations had tackled the tenacious problem of equity by facilitating more equitable distribution of services or by reporting to the public on extant inequities in service delivery. Many of the collaborations had engaged in advocacy work, with 36% involved in legislative changes, 31% involved in regulatory changes, and 36% involved in statewide efforts addressing early care and education policies.

Beyond fostering improvements in services and in the system of child care and early education, collaborations are asked to manage resources effectively. Of those investigated, 83% indicated they had used resources more effectively either by avoiding duplications in staff or services across programs or by increasing funds from public and private sources. The study indicates that nationally, collaborations are having impact. Though some concentrate on enhancing direct services and others on fostering system change, the study affirmed that collaborators were adept in fine-tuning their efforts to meet local and state need. (Individual collaborations are described in the Appendix.)

Data from this study confirm anecdotal findings of others and preliminary self-reports from collaborations in domains other than early care and education (Bruner, 1991). But clearly, far more research is needed on the outcomes of collaborative effort. Moreover, hard questions that have not yet been adequately addressed need attention. How do we know that collaborations are worth the effort? What is the cost-benefit of investing human and capital resources in collaboration? Given that collaboration is only one strategy in an array of alternatives to enhance service delivery (e.g., case management, co-location of programs), how do we judge its comparative effectiveness? Under what conditions is collaboration the most effective strategy?

WHEN DO COLLABORATIONS WORK BEST?

When the Context Is Fertile

Mounting data affirm that the context for collaboration is among the most important variables affecting collaborative formation and outcome. Melaville & Blank (1991) suggest that the social and political climate is the first factor likely to influence an interagency initiative. A supportive climate, one where the attitudes and priorities of the general public, key decision makers, and service providers support collaboration, is optimal. If positive working relationships predated the collaboration, so much the better. In contrast, a less favorable climate, one where a problem is not clearly identified or where key participants are preoccupied with other concerns, mitigates against successful collaborative work.

Kagan and colleagues (1990) suggest that a fertile context is necessary for effective collaboration to take root. Their analysis revealed that in addition to political and social contexts, historical, geographic, and ideological contexts are also critical. Collaborations are easier to initiate in settings where there is a history of collaboration over time. Conversely, in settings where historically the belief system has included the need for distinct power distribution among levels and branches of government, where federal and state guidelines are strictly interpreted, and where collaboration is seen as a threat to autonomy and accountability, collaborative productivity pales. Geographically, they found that rural areas are more receptive to collaboration, perhaps motivated by an acute paucity of resources or by the social isolation felt by rural practitioners. However, despite good intentions, geographic distance limits the effectiveness of many rural collaborations.

The importance of context cannot be underestimated as one of the critical variables influencing collaboration. At most, it may be that in settings where the context is not receptive, strategies other than collaboration should be carefully considered. At least, evaluating the context to assess its political, social, ideologic, geographic, and historic receptivity for collaboration is an important analytic step in launching any such effort.

When the Goals Are Clear

Collaborators identify the setting of clear and manageable goals as the most important step in launching a collaboration. Common vision unifies disparate parties and can serve as the vehicle for ironing out conceptual and practical differences. Underscoring the importance of establishing a unified vision, considerable attention has been devoted to the elements that constitute such a vision and the strategies that are most effective in achieving it. One helpful distinction has been offered by the Public/Private Ventures (1990) analysis of the National Alliance of Business' Compact Project (1989). It suggests that there are two types of vision. The first expresses the need for broad change. Such a vision helps to mobilize interest and keeps the collaborative endeavor from focusing too narrowly or from launching miniprojects that promise only marginal gain. The second vision is a practical vision that specifies major goals and objectives that the initiative must accomplish if the effort is to be successful. This distinction could also be described as "mobilizing" goals that are operative in early and preformation stages of collaboration and operational goals that more closely guide the day-to-day activities of the effort.

Achieving goal consensus has proven to be an undertaking of differing magnitude. In some communities, 2 years of work have been devoted to goal consensus, while in others it was achieved at the first meeting. Neither strategy is necessarily preferable. Interestingly, both those who arrived at goals quickly and those who laboriously constructed mission and goal statements often found they needed to revisit them frequently. Indeed, Kagan and colleagues (1990) found that most collaborations revisited their goals, either as a function of a standard annual review or progress evaluation, or as the result of a critical event. Most collaborations in this study reported "fiascos" or "aborted efforts" early on that necessitated goal modification. Rather than being felled by such events, the collaborations—so long as they remained open and flexible—were strengthened by them.

When Structure Matches Mission

Less well understood than the need for goal clarity and goal flexibility is the need for a collaboration to have an operational structure that matches its goals. The most common collaborative structure has been pictured as a circle whereby parties, typically representing different organizations, come together to determine mutually agreed-upon goals and strategies. But this is not collaboration's only structure. Many effective collaborations operate on what might be envisioned as a spoke, a structure whereby one agency or individual is at the hub and establishes a series of dyadic relationships with other groups. The spokes share a common commitment to enriching the hub but have little interaction separate from that organized or initiated by the hub.

A valid collaborative structure, the spoke works especially well for collaborations that aim to improve direct services (Kagan et al., 1990). Spokes can be efficient at marshaling resources and capitalizing on opportunities. Conversely, the analysis suggests that system-oriented collaborations function more optimally with a circle structure. While most voluntary collaborations allow their structure to be dictated by their goals, structure can be superimposed by mandate, irrespective of goal. Indeed, most mandates foster conditions that lead to a ring structure, which may conflict with the collaboration's mission or goals. To be maximally effective and efficient, collaborative structure must match collaborative intent.

When Mandate Is Facilitative, Not Restrictive

Though guided by good intentions, federal or state mandates have been regarded as detrimental by many collaborators. They were seen as impositions, and rather than facilitating local action, were often intrusive and counterproductive (Melaville & Blank, 1991).

Part of the dissatisfaction with a mandate is that it often is not accompanied by sufficient resources to carry out the tasks required. But collaborators also report that a mandate can limit goal formation and membership. While few of the collaborators in the Kagan and colleagues (1990) study disagreed with the mandated goals, many felt that they impeded the range of work undertaken and had a negative impact on the quality and quantity of outcomes. For example, some collaborations formed to meet the needs of children and families in crisis became so treatment oriented that they lost sight of prevention opportunities. Practitioners also expressed concern that mandated goals were so broad that they nearly "doomed" the collaboration to failure. Public/Private Ventures reported that virtually all the providers saw "mandated coordination as unrealistic and paper-producing" (1990, p. 45). Echoing these sentiments, Bruner (1989) suggests that what really matters in successful implementation is local capacity and will, highly idiosyncratic ingredients well beyond the reach of universal policy. In other words, you cannot mandate what really matters (McLaughlin, 1990).

On the other hand, mandates can be facilitative. They serve important start-up functions that can positively affect the collaboration. They help legitimize the collaborative endeavor, and they catalyze energy for the issues being addressed. In cases where dollars accompany the mandate, they perform a third function—financially supporting the collaboration.

Capitalizing on, but not being constrained by, mandate is the goal. To that end, mandates as we know them now need to be recontoured so that they offer maximum support at start-up and maximum flexibility during implementation. Mandates must accord more flexibility in goals, membership and structure, leaving fine-tuning and retuning to the collaborators.

When People Are Really Invested

Much has been written about leadership as a critical ingredient to effective organizations (see Chapter 4). The central proposition is that the leader must be a visionary, able to motivate, lead, support, affirm values, manage, and inspire. The question has also been raised as to whether leading a collaboration necessitates precisely the same skills as leading any organization. Is there something inherently different about collaboration that demands a new and perhaps different kind of leadership?

Collaborative leadership seems to involve all the skills necessary for leadership of any organization. But in addition, leaders of collaborations must also possess a strong ability to mobilize and to neutralize differences. Because of latent differences in intent and turf of collaboration members, the leader must be particularly adept at conflict resolution. Moreover, the leader must be sensitive to the conflicts that individual members face as they attempt to be true both to their home organization and to the collaboration. For these reasons, many leaders of collaborations emerge from outside the conventional service delivery system; they are often business or political leaders, able to commandeer respect for their abilities, access, and neutrality. Frequently such leaders have had broad-based backgrounds, training, and experience. Indeed, in the early care and education study (Kagan et al., 1990), few of the leaders were from the child care or early childhood field.

Much of the literature on collaborative leadership suggests that truly effective leadership occurs only when it is shared and nurtured. Terming this "servant leadership," Greenleaf (1977) contends that preparing others for leadership is as essential to successful leadership as leading itself. Such commitment to nurturing others seems particularly important in collaborations. This takes several forms. Often the original leader will select another to co-lead the endeavor. In the early care and education field, this is evidenced in collaborations initiated in conjunction with P.L. 99-457, where leadership is shared among practitioners and parents. In other settings, shared leadership is formally structured into the collaboration. For example, one early childhood effort in Florida has instituted a system of rotational leadership whereby one agency leads the collaboration in even-numbered years and the other, in odd-numbered years.

Perhaps the clearest expression of the concept of joint leadership is evidenced in those collaborations (about 20% of those in the Kagan and colleagues [1990] study) in which the initial leader consciously withdrew from titular leadership, assuming a back-seat role. In some cases, this role was akin to that of the "godfather"—rarely there, but ever present. In other cases, the originator was available for consultation but did not impose his or her views or goals on the new leader.

Collaborative endeavors demand special sensitivity to nurturing leadership and to empowering all members of the collaboration. Part of membership empowerment takes place in the selection and orientation process. At the very outset, members must see and feel that their participation is essential to the collaboration's success and beneficial to themselves and their organizations. They must feel that the collaboration is utilizing their expertise and also that they themselves are growing in the process. Part of the empowerment takes place through careful scrutiny of the allocation of responsibility. Careful orchestrating of objectives, assigning of tasks, and monitoring of communication empower collaborative members.

When Resources Are Available

The availability of resources and decisions regarding their utilization dramatically impact the effectiveness of any collaboration. Resources include, but are not limited to, dollars, staff, technology, and training.

Typically, collaborative finances are of two types: those used by the collaboration to finance its own activities (operating funds) and those administered by or through the collaboration to enhance services (project funds). Although some collaborations are run on a completely voluntary and unfunded basis, this is increasingly rare. For example, Kagan and colleagues (1990) found that a vast majority of service-oriented collaborations at the local and state level (93% and 89%, respectively) had stable operating funds. While the dollar amounts were not always large, the stability of the funding was critically important to the collaborative leaders because it enabled them to plan for the long term and consider priorities with a multiyear perspective. Project funds were more vulnerable, as were dollars to support system-oriented collaborations. Only 43% of the system-oriented collaborations at the state level had stable funds. This grave resource disparity between service- and system-oriented collaborations points out the particular challenge that system collaborations face and rationalizes the movement by system-oriented collaborations to adopt service missions as well.

These findings aside, the resource question remains problematic. The press for new collaborative dollars competes with the press for greater investments in human services. Gardner (1990) warns that tenacious collaboration alone will not make up for social underinvestment in children. And in some cases, collaboration must take a back seat to problems of greater or more pressing consequence. At the same time, though, Gardner (1990) suggests that without collaboration, such investments are unlikely to pay off.

Successful collaborations have staff or proxy staff as resources. Sometimes paid by the collaboration itself, sometimes paid by member organizations (frequently by simply swelling an already overdemanding job description), or sometimes completely voluntary, staff are the engines that keep the collaboration on track and mobile. Saved from burnout by their typically fierce dedication to task, collaboration staff need support, reinforcement, and nurturing. Often the position itself provides strong incentives; many regard these positions as offering tremendous growth opportunity and professional exposure. Nonetheless, collaborations need to be sensitive to staff exploitation and to provide incentives, including professional training and advancement opportunities.

When Process and Policies Are Clear

Little enhances effective collaboration as much as clear process and policies. Because collaborations are in the business of bringing together disparate entities, attention to process and policy is critical. Often agencies bring different operational styles, communication patterns, and experiences of decision making to the collaborative table. Without clear explication and agreement on the strategies to be used by the collaboration in these areas, time and energy will be diverted from the collaboration's primary goals to resolve process conflicts. Decisions to be mutually addressed include: How formal will the collaborative agreement be? Will it be written or verbally understood? How formal will the collaborative apparatus be? Will there be bylaws? What are the power limitations of an executive committee? Of the collaboration itself? How will routine (and emergency) communication be handled? What is considered privileged information? How confidential is confidential? How will differences in our ability to speak and understand one another's "languages" be handled? How will we move, as Melaville and Blank (1991) suggest, from "doubletalk" to plain talk?

In short, each collaboration is in the business of forming a new culture, distinct from that of its participant members. Part of the challenge lies in recognizing that collaboration is more than the amalgamation of its parts, that—even if it meets only twice a year—it is an organizational entity. Dedicating time and resources to establishing institutional practices is a necessary correlate of success.

WHAT COLLABORATIONS CAN*NOT* DO

It is necessary to maintain objectivity about collaboration as one listens to practitioners who have implemented successful collaborations and works with policy makers who regard collaboration as a social panacea (Kagan et al., 1990). This is particularly difficult because a "mythology" has enveloped collaboration. This mythology, festooned with glorious visions of improvements in the social condition, asks us to believe that: (1) collaboration can meet nonstop spiraling expectations for change; (2) collaboration is always a win-win scenario; and (3) a perfect strategy or model exists. These are patently false expectations, even for the most successful collaborations.

Nonstop, Spiraling Expectations for Change

In many ways, collaborations offer a dangerous optimism. Unlike the "change-agent" projects of the 1960s and 1970s, in which external experts came to change a "hostile" environment, collaborative efforts put the problem and the solution in the hands of those most vested in change. Recognizing the faults of the external change-agent strategy, now well documented in the literature, the collaborative participant strategy appears to counter previous mistakes. Current thinking suggests that when empowered and responsible for changing their own destiny, people do rise to the challenge. Collaboration is a vehicle that imbues participants with full responsibility for change.

In so doing, expectations of collaborative participants are raised, although not always met in practice. Sometimes the magnitude of the problem and its imbeddedness in the political or organizational context is not recognized by overzealous collaborators. Sometimes resources and structure, imposed externally, do not match the specified goals. And sometimes unpredictable events—union strikes, ousted incumbents—alter the best-laid collaborative plans. *What few understand is that collaboration is a microstrategy subjected to macroevents.*

Optimistic participants and policy makers can prepare themselves for inevitable setbacks if they understand that collaborations address problems that are chronic rather than acute, systemic rather than peripheral. Expectations must be realistic and circumscribed. Collaborations will not convert historic national support of individualism to enthusiasm for collectivism; they will not eradicate generations of social inequities; they will not transform social service delivery. Rather, they can reduce fragmentation; they can help make services more accessible for some children and parents; and they can bring a modicum of coherence to policy and planning. Data reveal that successful collaborations recognize the dangers that accompany false expectations and maintain equilibrium and ability to think broadly but realistically. They do not mistake volume for significance of activity or mission.

The Win-Win Scenario

Advocates of collaboration suggest that one of its strongest selling points is that it is always a win-win scenario. With representatives of different groups engaging in joint goal and strategy setting, collaborations create the aura of egalitarianism. And some manage to achieve this. But not all do.

Inherent contextual and status inequalities exist and may be exacerbated by collaboration. Child-care centers, because they tend to be small, economically fragile, and not a part of an established infrastructure, do not typically come to the collaborative table as equal players with schools. Nonschool personnel speak of "silent boundaries" that are not penetrated or "sacred cows" that are not discussed. In effect, collaborations are engaged in the challenge of reconciling a seemingly equitable process with inherent inequities. Collaborations can become zero-sum games with power, services, and resources remaining unequally distributed.

Understanding that collaborations do not eventuate in win-win situations for all players is not sufficient. Collaborators need to be sensitive to the potential losers and find vehicles to compensate for inequitable rewards that might ensue from collaboration. Helping collaborators see beyond their own agencies, turf, and programs is difficult in a bureaucratic context that rewards players for their dogged adherence to advancing single-agency aims. Helping people relinquish cherished and hard-fought-for turf for the common good is not easy. Collaborations need help understanding and dealing with the inevitable win–no-win situations that favor the whole over a particular agency. *Above all, we must come to grips with the knowledge that an improved system, not simply an improved agency, is necessary to assure desirable change for all.*

The Existence of a Perfect Strategy/Model

Collaborations are addressing many systemic and service challenges, but they are also creating another institutional layer. In some states collaborations have proliferated so rapidly under so many different auspices that megacollaborations are being considered. Order is needed as collaborations proliferate.

Equally as important as expansion in number is expansion in the variety of collaborations. There are many modes of collaboration. The lesson is not that collaborative strategies can be adopted, or even adapted, but that collaborations are distinct entities, microscopic reflections of the community and/or state ethos in which they exist. *Such mirroring of the extant culture suggests that collaboration is the inevitable and idiosyncratic interaction of the immediate climate—resources and capacity—and the historic receptivity to collaboration.* As such, collaborations remain infinite in variety, each a unique enterprise.

For true believers in the transportability of innovation or for advocates of the adaptation strategy, this is not good news. How much easier it would be if common barriers could be extracted from the experience of others or if "how-to" templates could be created for speedy replication. How lovely if the key ingredients of collaboration could be specified (as were program variables in the demonstration era) and then adapted in various locales. This is not the case. Collaborations are unique from the ground up; when maximally effective they reflect community attitudes, values, and mores. To expect commonality by overlaying national goals or mandating specific strategies is too simplistic an understanding.

Collaborations must be valued not for their applicability or transportability to other settings, but for their ability to empower localities and states to construct mechanisms to meet their own needs. Discrete examples of backward-mapping, of learning from practice to inform policy, collaborations are vehicles to understand how new institutional players and exciting organizational connections not routinely acknowledged in policy can be formed. Collaborations are not conventional strategies. As such, they both afford the opportunity and demand that we think about practice, policy, and research in innovative, even unconventional, ways.

CHAPTER 10

United We Stand:
Facing Future Issues

"When you go out into the world, watch out for traffic, hold hands
and stick together."

Robert Fulghum, 1990

IT IS TRUE. We need to hold hands and stick together, because today
America is at a critical juncture. Characterized by social and political
dichotomies, the nation faces economic globalization externally and
the economic bifurcation of society internally. While we play a preemi-
nent integrative role in the world order, in our own country the segregation of people and services runs rampant. "Incipient poverty," "the
permanent underclass"—concepts largely unknown a decade ago—
have become part of the national nomenclature. No longer are we
even horrified by the litany of crisp indicators that reflect our intellec-
tual and practical ignorance of social problems.

But those close to the human service industry understand the
urgency of America's domestic challenge. They realize that left unat-
tended, social problems will gag the economy and the nation in short
order. Armed with prognostications that verify these concerns and
with data that attest to the effectiveness and cost-effectiveness of preventive intervention programs, they understand that the time for action is now. But, reinforced by leaders from politics, business, and
industry, they also realize that what has worked in the past, while
important, may not necessarily work in the future. Business as usual
will only produce results as usual. And that is no longer sufficient.

Presaged by the long-understood reality of systemic inefficiency
and inequity, there is an undeniable desire to alter the basic system of
service delivery. Nothing short of a basic restructuring will enable
American social institutions to deal with the onslaught of social problems about to cascade on its doorsteps. Whether this restructuring is
dubbed the educational reform movement, social service case man-

agement, decategorization, or service integration, America is ripe for change.

Near the vortex of the groundswell for institutional reformation, collaboration has emerged as one recurrent theme. Reflecting a decided movement from a program to a system focus, collaboration has been discussed as the cornerstone of organizational innovation, school change, social networking, and welfare reform. And though less well understood than specific program interventions, collaborations have taken hold throughout the nation; they have become this era's social experiment. With little cross-fertilization and technical support, they have crafted approaches that seem to be working fairly well. And, building upon experience in the voluntary sector, public policy has responded by including provisions for collaboration in legislation.

Amidst the flurry of activity, collaborations are at a critical turning point. These highly idiosyncratic efforts can be left to their own devices. Without additional analysis or support, they can continue as social experiments, reminiscent of earlier eras. Some will no doubt be successful, leaving legacies for future generations to ponder. Others will fail. Alternatively, with analysis and support, America can garner lessons from the emerging natural laboratory of collaborations that may help reshape human service delivery.

With a focus on pioneering collaborations in early care and education, this volume has attempted to do the latter. But paradoxically, by reflecting on the past and investigating the present, this saga seems to have uncovered more questions than it has answered. Today's collaborations do raise provocative considerations that challenge conventional practice and thinking. Although our knowledge of them is far from complete, collaborations are still likely to flourish in this pivotal, albeit turbulent, era. Consequently, this volume closes by addressing difficult but unavoidable issues of practice, research, policy, and values.

PRACTICE ISSUES

The Challenge of Conceptualization and Expectation

The challenge of overcoming practical barriers to collaboration fills the literature as well as the experience of practitioners. Its pervasiveness suggests that perhaps some collaborative efforts have failed because of a narrowness of conceptualization. Focusing on the trees rather than the forest, advocates of collaboration may be reluctant to acknowledge or may fail to realize that their challenges are deeply embedded in the very system they are trying to reform. They see collaboration as a narrow intervention, akin to a single program. Experience suggests that effective collaborations envision their tasks broadly and strive to discern long-term consequences of their efforts. They recognize that, at the core, their work addresses fundamental issues: Can we alter priorities to be more child and family oriented? Can we focus on systems integrity *and* service quality when the norm has been a more unitary focus?

Effective collaborators seem to have grappled with the significance of their work and the idiosyncrasies of their context. They spend time understanding their history, geography, ideology, and political and social reality. They know that, in some cases, environments may not be receptive to collaboration. They know their best hope is to realistically evaluate contextual receptivity and to broaden the conceptualization of their *function*—although not necessarily their task. With thorough assessments and broad visions, collaborations can be launched even in hostile environments.

Collaborative work must also be tempered with reality. There may be communities or systems so impervious to change that collaboration, no matter how well conceptualized, will not succeed. Accepting that reality and seeking alternatives to collaboration is a far better strategy than expecting the impossible. America has had sufficient experience with overexpectation to understand its liabilities. We know that we should wear the shoe only if it fits.

Though appealingly tidy, the dilemma is that many communities will be left "shoeless." And in no small measure, these are likely to be precisely the communities that need the shoes most. What is the answer? Is collaboration a strategy doomed to fail those who need it most? Not necessarily. Still at an embryonic stage, collaboration needs nourishment and support to thrive. But once the understandings are more refined, the strategies more systematized, and the data more persuasive, the collaborative approach will become more institutionalized. With support for the concept and attention to efforts that facilitate it, even less supportive communities will be able to be moved.

The Challenge of Nourishment and Replenishment

What will it take to nourish and replenish collaboration? Effective collaboration involves complex skills and finely tuned sensitivities. Some people arrive at the collaborative portal naturally blessed with such. But the majority of us, trained in an educational system that applauded competition and discouraged collaboration, do not. For those trained in the field of early childhood, the dilemma is particularly acute. While we have been taught to foster creative problem solving, effective negotiation, and successful mediation among children, we have not been taught how to apply those skills to adults. Trist (1976), underscoring the magnitude of the problem, recognizes the differences between competitive and collaborative training as nothing short of a revolution, one for which our "revolutionaries" are sadly ill-prepared.

There are multiple solutions to the challenge. Taking a lesson from business and industry, which routinely train and retrain personnel for new responsibilities, we should launch inservice, skill-based training. Combining practical and theoretical work, such training would enable potential collaborative leaders to test their ideas and skills. Those less interested or less adept might decide to pursue other efforts, while those interested in pursuing leadership would be better equipped for the challenge at hand. Beyond inservice training, more preservice emphasis needs to be placed on cross-disciplinary training. In focusing on training, the field would be replenished.

But making training available is only part of the challenge; training must be appropriate to need. It seems that in the early care and education collaborative domain, practice is ahead of pedagogy. For example, we need to assess whether pedagogy amassed regarding systems change is appropriate in early care and education, a field that never conceptualized itself as a unified system. Moreover, the demonstration strategy used so frequently may be totally inappropriate in collaborative settings, with their highly idiosyncratic goals and missions. Indeed, it may be that new theories more appropriate to the era and the field might emerge from practice.

Because of the need to capitalize on the expertise that exists in today's collaborations, opportunities for networking and sharing experiences among collaborators are essential. Collaborators have routinely expressed concern that they are "flying by the seat of their pants" or "reinventing the wheel." Because their needs are immediate and their challenges complex, collaborators need the opportunity to share their successes, fiascos, and lessons. In so doing, collaborators are nourished.

Beyond training, collaborative enterprises will be nourished by financial resources. Experience indicates that if collaborations are to reach their potential, dollar resources sustained over time are necessary. The philanthropic community has been particularly supportive of service-oriented early care and education collaboratives. In contrast, system-oriented collaborations often are forced to wait at the legislative trough. Sometimes the wait is unduly long, as legislators are often wary of investing in collaboration because they fear it will add yet another layer of bureaucracy. Moreover, in times of scarce resources such expenditures often compete (usually unsuccessfully) with direct services requests. Complicating the issue further, many, though certainly not all, bureaucrats, wary of their turf (power and authority) being eroded, are only cautiously supportive. Overcoming the disparities between funding for service- and system-oriented collaborations is one goal; another is to require that *any* policy recommending collaboration be accompanied by the dollars to implement it.

RESEARCH ISSUES

Generating Research

Given the burgeoning number of collaborations and their freshness of approach, the time is ripe to expand our collective knowledge about the process and outcomes of contemporary collaboration.

Though the literature is filled with studies on process variables related to collaboration, today's efforts demand some reexamination of the issues. For example, our knowledge of the importance of contextual variables demands that we investigate more clearly the conditions that predate the establishment of collaborations. What is the role of individuals and institutions? How do real and perceived boundaries affect the launching of collaboration? What is the relationship between mandate and effectiveness? What various kinds of mandate exist?

Similar issues pertain to the developmental stages. Current collaborative work suggests that the stages may not be as linear or predictable as once envisioned. Given changing contextual conditions, including unstable financial and political support, many collaborations report decidedly different developmental trajectories. Research that investigates when and what factors accelerate and inhibit implementation would be helpful.

Conventional notions about leaders and followers may also be challenged by current collaborative work. What is the role of egalitarian leadership? Is it essential to effective collaborations? Should collaborations be broadly representative of the community, or does too diverse a representation impede effective functioning? How does membership turnover affect the collaboration? In short, if we are to utilize the experiences of 1990s collaborations as a base for improvement of the field, additional process research is necessary.

But, as suggested in the preceding chapter, there is also an urgent need to assess the outcomes of collaboration. Such an endeavor demands that researchers and practitioners together grapple with definitions of success. To hold collaborations accountable for, or to measure their success by, child and family outcomes remains problematic—a puzzle awaiting solution.

Utilizing Research

All too frequently quality research is produced but not used. This occurs because there is too little explicit attention accorded research dissemination and utilization. This is particularly true in the collaborative domain; limited research is being done, and even fewer systematic efforts are being made to disseminate research findings. Given that policies are being considered and practices are being envisioned, data from research would be most timely and helpful. To that end, renewed emphasis must be placed on effective dissemination efforts.

POLICY ISSUES

The Role and Function of Mandate

To date, most work has focused on de jure mandates—mandates of the law. We have seen that de jure mandates can inhibit collaboration by imposing too stringent requirements. Policy makers must realize the potential constraints and configure mandate to provide maximum flexibility. Such a strategy reflects current thinking about the need for bottom-up, as opposed to state, policy making. When policy makers understand that what really matters cannot be mandated (McLaughlin, 1990), they will find the way to create mandates that facilitate, rather than restrict, collaborations.

Future work needs to focus on de facto mandates, those that are not law but carry the weight of law. Buoyed by corporate or political support, such mandates may be even more potent than de jure mandates. Indeed, the historic success of voluntary collaborations suggests this might be the case.

What is certain is that the existence of mandate affects collaborations in very pervasive and direct ways. And because more states and locales are moving into the collaborative arena, it is imperative that we understand the different effects of de jure and de facto mandates and that we understand the elements from each that are transferable and that most promote collaboration.

Accountability and Community Capacity

The perpetual tug between state control and local autonomy characterizes collaborative work. Collaborations drawing state dollars must be accountable; on the other hand, they must not be so closely monitored or strictly regulated that they are not free to shape the effort to the contextual needs of the community. Collaborative policy must start with an assumption of local competence and a will to enhance local capacity. Particularly challenging given the desire of states to maintain control, collaboration must be recognized as a structured empowerment strategy, one whereby the balance of state and local authority and autonomy will be altered.

Segregating At-Risk Children

Currently, mandated collaborations are being advanced in legislation for at-risk children. Consequently, some collaborations are being established to serve primarily, and sometimes exclusively, at-risk children. Ironically, such efforts may exacerbate the segregated services they hoped to eliminate. Current and proposed legislation must accelerate the development of collaborations that join agencies serving all children. This may be accomplished by creating cross-agency and cross-sector incentives for collaboration or by eliminating regulations and restrictive program guidelines that impede collaboration. Because so much policy for young children focuses on and segregates at-risk youngsters, it is essential that steps be taken to facilitate collaboration across populations. To perpetuate collaboration among poverty-oriented agencies only minimizes the integrative potential of the collaborative enterprise.

VALUE ISSUES

America's institutions are steeped in its cultural values. Buoyed by a Constitution that preserves individual freedoms, America accords enduring social respect to the individual. We voice commitment to collective enterprise, but, as Grubb and Lazerson (1982) point out, our truly collective communities—the Shakers, the Amish, the Hasidic

Jews, and 1960s experimentalists—are considered deviant. Collectivism is a goal that "at least gives meaning to the historic search for community" (Grubb & Lazerson, 1982, p. 295). Nested in this ethos, contemporary collaborative efforts evoke a decided sense of naive idealism. They pale as meager efforts to transform a culture at odds with their basic beliefs. When all is said and done, collaborations will never be effective instruments of massive social reform, panaceas for all social problems. They will neither redress decades of social inequity nor alter America's deeply imbued passion for individualism.

But collaborations do offer some hope in early care and education. As literature and experience demonstrate, they can be one effective tool in inching the service delivery system along. We should be proud of those who have used collaboration to hasten higher-quality, more equitable, more accessible, or more comprehensive services for young children and their families. These people understand that the ultimate utility of collaboration is directly proportional to the social value accorded it.

VALUING COLLABORATION means valuing empowerment, growth, and diversity. It means moving from programmatic to systemic thinking, from short- to long-term visions. It means understanding that equity and access are conditions of quality, not factors ancillary to it. It means being realistic about what collaborations can accomplish within the context of deeply entrenched American institutions and deeply rooted American values. Above all, valuing collaboration means believing in and bringing out the best in *all* of America's children, families, and institutions. Armed with these values, we may all stand united.

Collaborations at Work

THE FOLLOWING DESCRIPTIONS are examples of the types of collaborations that can be found in cities, regions, and states throughout the nation.

Colorado

FAMILY EDUCATIONAL NETWORK OF WELD COUNTY
520 13th Ave., Greeley, CO 80631
Tere Keller   (303) 356-0600

Goals/Objectives. The network desires to improve the self-sufficiency of families and help parents to become active as their children's primary teachers.

History. The network began 17 years ago as a program under the auspices of the school district. Five years later, Weld County became the Head Start grantee and over time began to administer Head Start, Migrant Head Start, preschool programs and child care services for the Department of Social Services clients under the Family Support Act (FSA), and food services through the Commodity Supplemental Food Program.

Membership/Structure. The network staff is advised by a board of directors made up of all county commissioners and a Head Start policy council. Additionally, collaborative relationships exist with the public school and community groups.

Accomplishments. The network offers child-care services through Head Start, Migrant Head Start, the Colorado Preschool Project, and the FSA. The programs feature shared facilities, transportation, supplies, equipment, and consultant services. Many of the network's centers mix children in different programs, and all meet Head Start performance standards, regardless of funding. The policy council represents parents involved with all programs. Thus both children and parents are involved in ethnically and socioeconomically integrated activities. In collaboration with the Colorado AEYC, a community college, and a private foundation, training is offered to all teachers in the areas of certification, child development associate (CDA) training, and director training. Staff in all programs are offered full benefits and are compensated equitably.

Idaho

CHILD CARE CONNECTIONS
P.O. Box 6756, 1303 Fort St., Boise, ID 83707
Sharon Bixby   (208) 343-5437
   Goals/Objectives.   The agency seeks to promote the availability of quality, affordable child care.
   History.   In 1984, a community meeting sponsored by Northwest Area Foundation, and attended by representatives of churches, child-care, business, government, and community groups, identified local child-care issues and needs. As a result, a proposal to establish the agency was written and funded by Northwest Area Foundation.
   Membership/Structure.   Policy and operational decisions are made by an interagency administrative council, representing child-care agencies, schools, Head Start, private industry, community groups, legislators, and higher education. The council meets monthly, as do its subcommittees addressing resource development, public relations, and parent/provider services.
   Accomplishments.   The agency achieves its goals by (1) providing resource and referral services (R&R) to the public; (2) providing technical assistance to other R&Rs statewide, resulting in the establishment of three R&Rs in previously unserved areas; (3) the administration of child-care scholarships for low-income families; (4) consultation to employers that encourages employer involvement in child care; and (5) training and consultation to child-care providers. The agency has found that providers who use their services are twice as likely to remain in the field as providers who do not. Moreover, the agency has fostered community planning and coordination of services by sharing child-care supply and demand data with community groups, including private industry and the public schools. In collaboration with other child-care advocates, the agency successfully lobbied for local child-care center and family day-care licensing standards. With the local AEYC, the agency conducted a statewide survey of child-care provider salaries and co-sponsored activities and materials aimed at raising public awareness of provider professionalism.

Illinois

HUMAN SERVICES INSTITUTE
Chicago City-Wide College, 226 West Jackson, Chicago, IL 60606
Dr. Betty Hutchison   (213) 855-8225
   Goals/Objectives.   The institute (1) enhances program quality through provider training and operating model programs; (2) offers bilingual training to Hispanic centers and home providers; (3) provides preservice and inservice care to foster parents; and (4) provides parenting education to reduce abuse and neglect.

History. The institute coordinates academic programs in human services occupations, and runs six NAEYC accredited Child Development Centers serving children of staff, students, and the community. The centers are also training sites for City College's early childhood, nursing, and social service students. In addition, the institute has developed collaborative relationships with diverse outside groups through the outreach of institute staff.

Membership/Structure. The institute has developed collaborative programs with the Department of Human Services (DHS), the Department of Children and Family Services (DCFS), Chicago Board of Education, public and private colleges, universities, and social service and child welfare groups. Collaborative programs are advised by interagency groups, and communication is fostered through joint staff meetings and active participation in advisory groups of collaborators.

Accomplishments. Through CDA and bilingual CDA programs offered in collaboration with DHS, the institute develops in providers a sense of professionalism. Through collaboration with the Chicago Board of Education, the institute has become a subcontractor to run pilot programs for at-risk students. Through the Foster Parent Program offered in collaboration with DCFS, potential candidates are trained and inappropriate parents are screened out. The program's success has resulted in the design of a variety of inservice programs for foster parents, including one on caring for drug-exposed infants.

VOICES FOR ILLINOIS CHILDREN
53 West Jackson, Suite 515, Chicago, IL 60604
Jerome Stermer   (312) 427-4080

Goals/Objectives. The agency's overall objective is to improve the lives of Illinois children. Each year, specific objectives are set; currently, work is being done on the implementation of an Early Intervention Program, income tax credit for low-income families, and a report and analysis of the state's pilot preschool program. On each issue, the agency collaborates with other concerned groups.

History. In 1986, with funding from the Chicago Community Trust, a task force of business and community leaders was formed to do a state-level needs assessment and make recommendations regarding the provision of services to children. The task force's conclusion was that no one agency alone could address all issues; therefore, in 1987, the agency was formed to do research, advocacy, and promotion of collaboration.

Membership/Structure. Staff of the agency are advised by a board of directors representing private industry, community and public service groups, schools, a hospital, advocacy groups, the University of Illinois, and the courts. Committees address operational issues as well as specific projects and outreach activities for children's groups statewide.

Accomplishments. Publication of newsletters and a 1990 *Children's Agenda* keep the public and policy makers informed about children's issues.

Additionally, the agency addresses the following concerns in collaboration with state government, advocates, parents, and service providers: (1) increasing funding for preschool programs, abuse/neglect prevention programs, and low-income day care; (2) increasing accessibility of early intervention programs; (3) creating a state Child Find program; (4) creating scholarships to increase the pool of qualified early intervention professionals; and (5) establishing uniform provider salaries and licensing requirements among Head Start, day care, and school-based preschool programs.

Iowa

CHILD AND FAMILY POLICY CENTER
100 Court Ave., Suite 312, Des Moines, IA 50309
Senator Charles Bruner   (515) 243-2000

Goals/Objectives. The center seeks to provide stronger links between public policy makers and research on issues affecting children and their families by (1) developing recommendations to meet the needs of at-risk children and prevent future welfare dependency and (2) providing technical assistance, oversight, and support to state program initiatives.

History. The center was initiated in 1989 as a result of Senator Bruner's perception that public policy was insufficiently tied to research on child development and sociology. Thus, he formed the center as a clearinghouse of information for policy makers.

Membership/Structure. The center is served by a state board representing state and private universities, business, and labor. This group helps set state policy on children and families by (1) identifying state needs, (2) tracking demographic trends to predict future needs, and (3) linking research and public policy to help determine what research is needed to support policy making. A national advisory board advises on grants written by the center and helps identify potential funding sources. It represents researchers, advocates, and child development scholars.

Accomplishments. The center has published (1) *Iowa's 1988 Legislative Initiatives: Assisting At-Risk Youth and Families*, an effort to provide technical assistance to schools developing grant programs; (2) the *Proceedings* of the center's workshop for recipients of the state's family development grant program, Iowa's major effort to integrate welfare reform with child development; (3) guides to collaboration, including a chapter in the National Conference of State Legislature's *Family Policy* book and a paper for the Association for Public Policy Analysis and Management; and (4) *Improving Maternal and Child Health: A Legislator's Guide*, a book for state policy makers on possible program initiatives to improve child health.

IOWA CHILD DEVELOPMENT COORDINATING COUNCIL
Department of Education, Grimes State Office Building, Des Moines, IA 50319-0146

Dr. Carol Alexander Phillips   (515) 281-7844; Ms. Susan Andersen
(515) 281-4747

Goals/Objectives.   The council has been charged with (1) developing a definition of *at-risk*; (2) establishing minimum guidelines for comprehensive child development services; (3) developing a biennial inventory of child development services; (4) making recommendations regarding curriculum and staff qualifications; (5) awarding grants for programs that provide services to at-risk children; (6) encouraging submission of grant requests from all types of providers of child development services; and (7) submitting recommendations to the legislature on state child development services.

History.   The council was established in 1988 by legislative mandate.

Membership/Structure.   The council's members, who are appointed by public agencies, include representatives of the Departments of Education, Human Rights, Human Services, and Public Health. The council meets monthly, and subcommittees meet as needed.

Accomplishments.   The council has (1) increased direct services to children and families statewide; (2) expanded services to parents, including GED, literacy, and CDA training; (3) increased access to services by providing transportation; (4) improved quality of services by funding programs that have appropriate child/teacher ratios, conducted self-studies, offered enhanced staff training, and provided comprehensive services by linking with other programs; (5) fostered links among local programs and the state's Maternal and Child Health initiative; (6) encouraged Local Early Childhood Advisory Committees to expand representation to coordinate services of Head Start and child care as well as school-based programs; (7) created databases at state and local levels to provide coordinated information to parents, providers, and policy makers; and (8) instituted local early childhood committees to foster collaborative community planning and needs assessments.

Kentucky

VIRGINIA PLACE
College of Home Economics, University of Kentucky, 102 Erikson Hall,
Lexington, KY 40506-0050
Dean Peggy S. Meszaros   (606) 257-2878

Goals/Objectives.   The goal of the program is to help families become self-sufficient.

History.   Plans for Virginia Place began to be discussed in 1984 by county government officials, the university, and Tenant Services staff. In an effort to break the cycle of poverty so evident in the city, Virginia Place was opened in 1986 as a transitional program to support single-parent families while parents pursue their education and acquire employment.

Membership/Structure.   The program is collaboratively provided by the colleges of education, nursing, and home economics of the University of Kentucky, whose faculty and students donate their time and expertise. An executive board meets monthly, made up of board co-presidents, each of the deans of the three colleges, and other staff. A working board meets every 2 months and represents university faculty, private business, and the mayor's office.

Accomplishments. The program is the only model in the nation of an academically guided program for self-sufficiency. Housing is provided to participants, as well as on-site health services, financial counseling, nutrition education, individual and family counseling, and child care meeting NAEYC guidelines. School-age children receive afterschool tutoring, and transitions are planned between Virginia Place's child-care program and the public schools. An interdisciplinary case management team conducts family assessments and makes referrals to off-site services as needed. The program succeeds in supporting families for a transitional time, during which they acquire the education and employment to become self-sufficient.

Massachusetts

COMMUNITIES UNITED, INC.
111 Mt. Auburn St., Watertown, MA 02172
Ann Linehan   (617) 923-2010

Goals/Objectives. The agency serves preschool children through providing Head Start and subsidized child-care services and through expanded social and health services in collaboration with community organizations.

History. Communities United was founded in 1970 by a group of parents as a Head Start grantee. Since 1982, it has served nine communities through providing and coordinating early childhood services.

Membership/Structure. Staff of the agency are advised by a Health Advisory Committee, Head Start Policy Council, and an interagency board of directors, which meets monthly and represents parents, schools, local government, social service organizations, private industry, and parents.

Accomplishments. The agency provides interagency team assessments of children in its programs, with referrals made to needed services. Using the services of interpreters from social service agencies, the agency assists non-English-dominant parents to access outside services. Monthly parent meetings are attended by school and social service agency staff, who inform parents about the services available; the agency arranges parent visits to community agencies. With the public schools, the agency has established a Collaboration for Children Project, a program designed to develop transitions for special needs children between early intervention programs and public schools. It has opened day-care centers in public housing projects in collaboration with the state Housing Authority. A database on children served and services provided eases transitions between programs. The agency participates in joint program and funding planning with social service agencies and other early childhood groups.

MASSACHUSETTS EARLY CHILDHOOD ADVISORY COUNCIL

Department of Education, Bureau of Early Childhood Programs, 1385
Hancock St., Quincy, MA 02169
Sandra Putnam Franklin, Interagency Coordinator   (617) 770-7434;
Elisabeth Schaefer, Bureau Director   (617) 770-7476

Goals/Objectives.   The council (1) advises the state board of education
on early childhood issues; (2) reviews early childhood program evaluation,
certification, and program standards; and (3) supports state and local interagency initiatives.

History.   Two earlier groups [an Early Childhood Advisory Council, established by the Public School Improvement Act (Chapter 188) to award grants
to schools offering child-care services, and an interagency council administering special education funds] merged in 1988 and became the present Early
Childhood Advisory Council.

Membership/Structure.   Council members meet bimonthly and represent the public schools, child care, Head Start, advocacy groups, parents, the
Office for Children, higher education, and the Departments of Social Services, Public Health, Public Welfare, Mental Retardation and Mental Health.
Subcommittees address public awareness, integration of children with special
needs, teacher certification and professional qualifications, parent involvement and family education, future trends in early childhood education, children whose first language is not English, and transitions for children from
early intervention programs to the public schools and Head Start through the
Collaboration for Children Project.

Accomplishments.   The council has developed program standards for
grants awarded to local school districts for planning and operating early childhood programs. To be funded, programs must demonstrate collaboration with
community and school groups, parent involvement, staff development opportunities, and high quality curricula. To encourage school-community collaboration, the council has published a guide to establishing local interagency
advisory councils, a report on the role of public schools in child care, and case
studies of successful Chapter 188 and Collaboration for Children Programs.

HEAD START PLUS

Montachusett Opportunity Council, Inc., 26 Main St., Leominster, MA 01453
Mae Beth Skidmore   (508) 537-9547

Goals/Objectives.   Head Start Plus seeks to increase access to vocational skills training and good employment for Head Start parents, thereby making parents self-sufficient and increasing the entire family's well-being.

History.   Head Start Plus began as a result of perceived needs on the
part of its two major partners. The Montachusett Regional Vocational Technical School was interested in offering adult training. Head Start had been
operating an extended day program for its parents who were participating in
work training through the Department of Public Welfare, but participation

was disappointing. The two applied for federal and state collaborative vocational technical funds, and the program began in the 1988–1989 school year.

Membership/Structure. An interagency advisory committee oversees the program. Monthly meetings are attended by representatives of Head Start, the Montachusett Opportunity Council Learning Center, the vocational technical school, and a parent.

Accomplishments. As a result of the program, Head Start parents who participate impart a sense of stability to the school classes and activities and Head Start's extended day program is more fully utilized. Through networking efforts with local businesses, graduates of Head Start Plus are successfully placed in jobs. Head Start and vocational education funds are combined to offer full-day child-care services on the Head Start model. Sick child care is offered to children of participants through a collaborative relationship with the county hospital, keeping parent absenteeism low. The Montachusett Opportunity Council provides help with homework, tutoring, and remedial education through its learning center. Transportation is provided to parents between the Head Start center, the school, and the learning center.

Michigan

MICHIGAN COMMUNITY COORDINATING CHILD CARE ASSOCIATION
2875 Northwind Dr., Suite 200, East Lansing, MI 48823
Mark Sullivan   (517) 351-4171

Goals/Objectives. The collaboration's goals are to (1) coordinate and support delivery of services on a local level; (2) coordinate and improve development of policy on a state level; and (3) identify, obtain, and manage funds to improve child care across the state.

History. The Michigan Community Coordinating Child Care Association (4C) was originally established in 1972 by the governor as a technical assistance and administrative umbrella for the local 4C. In 1980, because of fiscal constraints, funding for the organization was cut. The organization was reestablished in 1987 as a result of the recommendations of the Michigan Women's Commission.

Membership/Structure. Membership is made up of the local 4Cs, who represent child-care providers, parents, community agencies, policy makers, city council members, and the business community. An advisory committee representing parents, unions, business, child-care providers, and the Departments of Public Health, Mental Health, Social Services, Education, and Labor meets quarterly to provide program direction.

Accomplishments. The organization has published a report on child-care services in Michigan, successfully advocated for $23 million in state funds for implementing an At-Risk 4-Year-Old Program, and provided CDA scholarships. Additionally, the organization provides child-care information to its affiliates, conducts statewide child-care recruitment and training with funds from Mervyn's Dayton/Hudson and the Ford Foundation, and participates in collaborative efforts to increase the availability and affordability of child care with the Governor's Task Force on Child Care, the Child Care Employee Project of San Francisco, the Michigan Association for the Education of Young Children, and other consumer/advocacy groups.

Minnesota

CHILD CARE RESOURCE & REFERRAL, INC.
2116 Campus Dr. SE, Rochester, MN 55904
Tutti Sherlock   (507) 287-2020

Goals/Objectives.   The agency provides referral to child-care and pre-school programs, financial assistance for child care, early childhood training, and support services to the preschool community. Additionally, the agency fosters community collaboration by informing the community of deficiencies and problems in the child-care service delivery system and catalyzing community groups to work together for change.

History.   In 1970, a study of child care in Olmsted County recommended that a child care communications system be established. In 1972, Olmsted Council for Coordinated Child Care, Inc. (4C) began operation; in 1980, 4C became Child Care Resource & Referral.

Membership/Structure.   The agency provides child-care referral to the public and to employers and handles all public child-care funding, including that for Family Support Act initiatives, nursery school scholarships, child-care and preschool services, Head Start, Parents Anonymous, parent counseling, the child-care food program, provider training, and work/family seminars. Staff are advised by a board of directors, which represents parents, private industry, and various community groups.

Accomplishments.   As a management agency for all public child-care funding in the community, the agency provides a central point of access for all families eligible for these services. Most recently, the agency has (1) expanded its R&R activities; (2) created a Care for Two Program, registering caregivers who will provide care for the children of one other family; (3) expanded Head Start to include a center-based program and to increase the number of families served; (4) implemented a regional Child Care Training Project; (5) expanded the child-care food program; and (6) collaborated with other community groups to increase the supply of infant care and establish afterschool care programs, among other initiatives to promote community planning and collaborative problem solving.

PARENTS IN COMMUNITY ACTION, INC.
4225 Third Ave. South, Minneapolis, MN 55409
Alyce Dillon   (612) 823-6361

Goals/Objectives.   The agency seeks to empower parents to be their children's primary teachers and to assist families in becoming self-sufficient.

History. The agency was formed by Head Start parents who were dis-satisfied with the parental involvement opportunities offered by the public schools. Catalyzing community support, the group became a Head Start grantee in 1971. Since that time, the agency has collaborated with community groups to enhance its services to low-income children.

Membership/Structure. Interagency agreements with outside groups specify program oversight by joint advisory committees or by specific staff from the collaborating agencies who are responsible for the collaborative pro-grams.

Accomplishments. The agency participates in mutual screenings and referrals and coordinates services with many community health and social service groups. Additionally, with the public schools, the agency has devel-oped a transitional kindergarten program called High Five for children eligible for Head Start. The program involves coordination of services and joint staff-ing by Head Start and school personnel. The agency owns and operates an Early Childhood Family Development Center, which houses a Head Start center and several other programs for young children and their families, al-lowing a single point of access for families needing child-care, health, mental health, and support services. The agency has written, with the Greater Min-neapolis Daycare Association, a guide to collaboration called *Head Start Link-ages: Establishing Collaborative Agreements*.

UNITED WAY'S SUCCESS BY 6
United Way of Minneapolis Area, 404 South 8th St., Minneapolis, MN 55404
Beverly Propes   (612) 340-7686

Goals/Objectives. The collaboration seeks to build community aware-ness and understanding of early childhood development issues, improve ac-cess to services for all families with young children, and encourage private-public collaboration.

History. The collaboration was formed in January 1988, shortly after a new United Way strategic plan mandated the organization become more ag-gressively involved in collaborations to address serious problems facing the community. The CEO of Honeywell simultaneously pledged his involvement and commitment to early childhood issues.

Membership/Structure. Approximately 250 volunteers support the ini-tiatives of 15 committees. Chairs of 14 subcommittees serve on a Management Committee of volunteers, which oversees the program's operations and re-ports to the United Way board of directors. The Partners Group represents 40 public, private, and nonprofit institutions involved in family/children services and advocacy efforts, and advises Success by 6.

Accomplishments. The collaboration has (1) coordinated and devel-oped a full advertising campaign, as well as conducted community forums and various activities to raise public awareness of the importance of early childhood development; (2) encouraged business leaders to testify before the legislature on early childhood issues and, in collaboration with others, obtained $35.6 million in additional support for young children; (3) encouraged the Education Committee of the Chamber of Commerce to sponsor an initiative helping Chamber members to resolve workforce concerns pertaining to work-family conflicts; (4) established a prenatal home visit and family support program for families with young children involving 35 human service agencies coordinated in agreement with the Minneapolis Youth Coordinating Board; and (5) funded $250,000 in development and distribution of child-rearing and educational materials for parents and providers.

Missouri

METROPOLITAN COUNCIL ON CHILD CARE MID-AMERICA REGIONAL COUNCIL
600 Broadway, 300 Rivergate Center, Kansas City, MO 64105
Roberta Ezell, Council Coordinator; Stacie G. Goffin, Chairperson
(816) 474-4240

Goals/Objectives. The council was created to serve as a catalyst for the development of an effective, high-quality early childhood care and education *system* in metropolitan Kansas City.

History. The council was formally established in January 1989 as an outgrowth of a community-based task force formed to study and make recommendations for improving child care in the metropolitan community. In June 1990, the council received funding covering a 5-year period from the Ewing Marion Kauffman Foundation, the Hall Family Foundations, and the Junior League of Kansas City, Missouri.

Membership/Structure. The council is sponsored by the Mid-America Regional Council (MARC), a voluntary association of local governments serving the bistate Kansas City metropolitan area. The council receives extensive support from MARC staff; as of January 1991, a full-time coordinator was hired. The council itself is comprised of approximately 25 community representatives from local governments, labor, the Chamber of Commerce, the civic, corporate, and foundational communities, the media, appointees by the governors of Missouri and Kansas, and early childhood representatives from public schools and public and private (both profit and not-for-profit) programs. Equally diverse membership is found among the 100 individuals serving on the council's five coordinating subcommittees, which work to help accomplish the council's mission in the areas of professional development, advocacy, public awareness, resource and referral, and school-aged child care.

Accomplishments. In addition to securing funding commitments for the next 5 years, establishing itself as an important community voice on the issue of early childhood care and education, and involving more than 100 individuals who represent the diverse constituencies in early childhood education in the council's efforts, the council has (1) begun to organize itself as a central voice for advocacy on issues relevant to early childhood education; (2) created a quarterly calendar of short-term, low-cost training opportunities for area child-care teachers and family day-care providers; (3) developed a speakers bureau to inform the community about the council and relevant issues; (4) prepared a report on local zoning regulations related to child care and shared the information with more than 100 cities and counties in the metropolitan area; (5) prepared a report on before- and afterschool child-care programs offered on school district properties in the eight-county region that was distributed to superintendents and others in the 53 school districts in the metropolitan community; (6) drafted a long-term career plan for early childhood professions and initiated work on how this plan might be implemented in the community; (7) developed and distributed a brochure and public service announcement on resource and referral services available to parents in the metropolitan area; and (8) begun to organize a comprehensive survey to collect information on compensation issues, the availability of nonpublic school care for children with special needs, and existing levels of professional preparation.

ST. LOUIS ALLIANCE FOR BETTER CHILD CARE

5082 Westminster Pl., St. Louis, MO 63108
Lori Geismar-Ryan   (314) 725-1350

Goals/Objectives. The alliance's objectives are to collaborate on advocacy efforts to pass the Act for Better Child Care and to create a collaborative advocacy network by bringing together local groups and local chapters of national organizations with a focus on children and families.

History. The alliance grew out of the NAEYC 1987 national conference, which addressed passage of the ABC bill and the joint NAEYC/public broadcasting documentary, *Who Cares for the Children?* In response to the call for grass-roots advocacy for ABC, the St. Louis AEYC public policy committee created the alliance.

Membership/Structure. Members represent St. Louis AEYC, Child Welfare League, National Council of Jewish Women–St. Louis Chapter, Child Daycare Association, Junior League, and city and state government. Other interested parties, such as Head Start and the Urban League, are on the mailing list. The group meets two or three times a year, with dissemination of information through mailings and by phone.

Accomplishments. Members share resources to support one another's advocacy efforts; for instance, the St. Louis Chapter of the National Council of Jewish Women made funds available to the St. Louis AEYC to partially support production of a video on the community's day-care needs. All members share data to allow for effective testimony and preparation of public fact sheets on day care. Because of their involvement with the alliance, members who provide direct services have successfully involved parents and day-care staff in advocacy efforts. The alliance is recognized as an important group, and its input is solicited by national and state legislators and advocates. Members testify often. The alliance successfully presented the views of the St.

Louis community regarding the importance of state regulations applying to all day-care centers, including church-sponsored ones.

Montana

EARLY CHILDHOOD PROJECT
Herrick Hall, Montana State University, Bozeman, MT 59717
Billie Warford   (406) 994-3241

Goals/Objectives. The goal of the ECP is to improve the quality and availability of services to young children and their families in Montana through collaborative efforts of agencies, organizations, and individuals concerned about children.

History. The project began in 1985 with funding from the Northwest Area Foundation. The president and founder of the Montana Association for the Education of Young Children initiated a state-level collaboration with the Montana Child Care Association and the Department of Family Services, along with other child advocates.

Membership/Structure. The collaboration includes representation from the above organizations and the Office of Public Instruction. The Indian Child Welfare Services is also interested in being included. The collaboration publishes a newsletter five to six times a year that is distributed to more than 2,000 early childhood care and education professionals, advocates, and agency personnel as funding permits.

Accomplishments. The project has published the *Montana Early Childhood Resource Directory, Montana Child Care: Questions and Answers 1988*, and *Dependent Care Assistance Options: A Guide for Montana Employers*; facilitated the Governor's Conference on Employer Supports for Child Care; developed a booklet on "Guidelines for Opening a Preschool in Montana"; conducted a market rate survey; and produced a video on "Taking Care of Montana's Children."

MONTANA ALLIANCE FOR BETTER CHILD CARE
10 West Cleveland, Bozeman, MT 59715
Billie Warford   (406) 587-7431

Goals/Objectives. The alliance seeks to (1) foster interagency cooperation in identifying the needs and finding solutions for quality child care; (2) improve public awareness concerning the importance of quality, affordable, accessible child care; and (3) organize member groups to affect local and state policy decisions at a grass-roots level for the improvement of child care.

History. The alliance grew out of a previously established collaboration, the Early Childhood Project, based at Montana State University. Because of its campus affiliation, it was difficult for the project to address public policy issues. In 1987, the project used foundation funding to hire a consultant to assess the policy needs of the state and make recommendations about who should be involved with the group. Six months later, the alliance was formed.

Membership/Structure. Members represent private industry, child care providers, R&Rs, the AEYC, higher education, advocacy groups, social service agencies, and state government. An interagency board makes policy decisions and meets frequently when the legislature is in session. The entire membership meets regularly at the State Early Childhood Conference.

Accomplishments. The alliance has successfully created and passed legislation that (1) designates the Department of Family Services as the lead agency in Montana for child-care issues; (2) creates the Governor's Advisory Council on Child Care to study the current child-care delivery system and make recommendations to the legislature; (3) creates and provides funding for a statewide child care R&R network; (4) provides tax credits for employer investment in child care; and (5) removes a freeze on the state reimbursement rate for child care.

YELLOWSTONE COUNTY HEAD START, INC.
P.O. Box 2056, Billings, MT 59103
Judy Bryngelson   (406) 245-7233

Goals/Objectives. The agency's objective is to provide high-quality, comprehensive services to children aged 4 and 5.

History. The Yellowstone County Head Start began as a community services group 25 years ago. Beginning in 1986, collaborative relationships developed with two school districts, the Department of Agriculture, and other early childhood groups as a result of the outreach of Head Start staff.

Membership/Structure. Collaborative programs are advised by individual, interagency advisory groups. Currently, Head Start and its school and community partners are applying for a corporate grant to employ a full-time coordinator of the collaborative programs.

Accomplishments. Collaboration with schools has allowed (1) the establishment of a special education resource room in a Head Start center for handicapped Head Start children; (2) evaluations and speech therapy for Head Start children; (3) full-day child care on the Head Start model through a joint Even Start grant; (4) attendance at school parent meetings by Head Start staff; (5) joint training and staff meetings, as well as shared materials and supplies; and (6) transition planning to kindergarten. Collaboration with the Department of Agriculture has provided nutrition counseling for Head Start and school staff and parents.

New Hampshire

CHILD AND FAMILY SERVICES OF NEW HAMPSHIRE
99 Hanover St., Manchester, NH 03101
Kim Dean-Valdez   (603) 668-1920

Goals/Objectives. The agency seeks to increase the supply of affordable day care.

History. The agency was established in 1850 as the City Missionary Society, providing services to the poor. Many years ago, the agency provided day care to the children of mill workers. Its recent involvement in day care began in 1987, with a state grant to study local employers' attitudes toward day care and initiatives in employer-supported day care, R&R, provider recruitment, and advocacy.

Membership/Structure. The agency collaborates with the New Hampshire Charitable Fund, Chambers of Commerce, the Governor's Office, the Department of Health and Human Services, the legislature, day-care providers and advocates, the Family Daycare Association, and Child Care R&R Network.

Accomplishments. With the Chamber of Commerce, the agency developed a brochure and co-sponsored a seminar on employer-supported day care, resulting in nine Manchester employers initiating employee day-care benefits. With the legislature, New Hampshire Business & Industry Association, and many others, the agency coordinated a statewide conference on employer-supported day care attended by representatives of 400 businesses. With the State Office of Economic Services, it established funding for a Family Daycare Association and recruitment project. With the Association, the agency offers start-up advice, training, and grants to home providers for equipment and home refurbishment. With the Mayor's Committee on Child Care, the agency created a Child-Care Coordinator position, funded by the city and housed at the agency. With the New Hampshire Charitable Fund and the State Daycare Advisory Committee, the agency developed a 5-year day-care plan for the state. With the Child Care R&R (CCR&R) Network of New Hampshire and the Division of Public Health, the agency is developing an operating manual, standards, and newsletter for CCR&R in the state, and will develop a statewide school-age child-care council.

New Jersey

EMERGENCY COMMITTEE TO SAVE CHILD CARE
43 Hill St., Newark, NJ 07102
Trish Morris   (201) 643-3710

Goals/Objectives. The committee provides resources to day-care teachers and administrators and advocates on child-care issues on the local, state, and national levels.

History. The committee was initiated in 1974 by a group of nonprofit day-care providers who were concerned about the proposed use of state and federal funds to start up new child-care centers. The committee successfully lobbied for funds to be used for upgrading and refurbishment of existing centers. Though no formal decision was made to prolong the committee's existence, it has remained intact for 16 years to address local and state child-care concerns.

Membership/Structure. Committee membership now includes both nonprofit and for-profit day care, Head Start, and parents. Additionally, the committee collaborates with the schools, the Newark Office for Children, the Federation of Youth Services, health and social service agencies, and businesses. It meets quarterly.

Accomplishments. The committee has successfully lobbied to avert city cuts in funds supporting school-age child care and to create a Child Care Network R&R service within the Newark Office for Children. The committee participates on a state policy development board by setting and revising child-care regulations and conducts a joint needs assessment with the Newark Office for Children and the Federation of Youth Services. Committee members are in the process of establishing a Teacher Training Program and developing a comprehensive health plan to be shared by child-care centers.

NEW JERSEY CHILD CARE ADVISORY COUNCIL
c/o Office of Child Care Development, Department of Human Services, CN 700, Trenton, NJ 08625
Dr. Edna Ranck, Coordinator   (609) 984-5321

Goals/Objectives. The council has been charged with (1) reviewing child-care center rules and regulations; (2) advising on child-care needs and policies; (3) studying and recommending alternative child-care resources; and (4) facilitating employer-sponsored child care through information and technical assistance.

History. The council was created by state legislation, the Child Care Center Licensing Act, in 1983.

Membership/Structure. Members represent Head Start, child care, schools, parents, social services, children's advocacy groups, National Black Child Development Institute (NBCDI), the New Jersey AEYC, the Puerto Rican Daycare Association, state-sponsored R&Rs, private industry, higher education, the Departments of Human Services, Community Affairs, Commerce and Economic Development, Education, Health, and Labor, the Divisions of Youth and Family Services and Women, and the Office of Child Care Development (DHS).

Accomplishments. The council has contributed to the development and implementation of legislation that created (1) an intergenerational childcare program in the Division on Aging; (2) relief from zoning restrictions on family day-care homes; (3) a survey of child-care needs of state employees; (4) grants for school-aged child care; and (5) voluntary family day-care home registration. The council wrote and presented to the legislature a comprehensive plan for child care in the state, which resulted in (1) legislation for a loan and grant program to start, expand, and renovate child-care centers; (2) expansion of public R&Rs statewide; and (3) development of a common computerized database on child-care services. The council revised center regulations with an Ad Hoc Citizens Advisory Committee and successfully advocated for an increase of $2 million in the Social Service Block Grant (SSBG) budget for center staff salaries.

URBAN PREKINDERGARTEN PILOT PROGRAM
Division of General Academic Education, New Jersey State Department of
Education, 225 West State St., CN 500, Trenton, NJ 08625
Tynette W. Hills   (609) 984-3429

Goals/Objectives.   The program was initiated to prepare impoverished
urban children for success in school and to counteract patterns of early and
continuing academic failure.

History.   The program came about by the direction of the governor to
the commissioners of the Departments of Education and Human Services.
The program was planned in 1988–1989 and implemented in 1989–1990. Local
pilot programs will operate until 1992, when an evaluation report and recommendations will be presented to the governor and the legislature. Currently,
local programs that meet established guidelines are operated in three urban
communities by either local public school systems or Head Start agencies.

Membership/Structure.   A state interagency management team awards
funds and monitors local pilot programs; members represent the Departments of Education and Human Services. The team meets formally twice a
month and communicates informally between meetings. Additionally, an advisory committee made up of groups broadly representative of the early childhood community meets three times a year. The state interagency management
team offers technical assistance on site and in conferences twice a year, attended by all local program staff.

Accomplishments.   Full-day programs serve previously unserved children with comprehensive services in health, nutrition, education, social services, and parent involvement opportunities. Extended child care is available
for those who need it. Continuity of experience is provided by learning activities that are linked to prior achievements and are continuous from year to
year. Careful transitions to kindergarten are planned.

New York

CHILD CARE RESOURCE DEVELOPMENT PROGRAM
Alumni Hall, Elmira College, Box 855, Elmira, NY 14901
Ellen Wohl   (607) 734-3941

Goals/Objectives.   The program endeavors to increase available, affordable, quality child care through providing, promoting, and coordinating comprehensive quality day-care services.

History.   Originally the Elmira Daycare Center in 1965, the program
soon became a Head Start grantee and later, in 1977, expanded to offer subsidized child care. In 1985 it developed a training program for family day-
care providers and in 1987, under a state and local Department of Social
Services contract, implemented child-care resource and referral services.
Longstanding collaborative relationships exist with other community service
organizations.

Membership/Structure.   The program is sponsored by the Chemung

County Child Care Council, a group widely representative of all groups with interest and involvement in child care. Additionally, collaborative groups meet to coordinate collaborative programs. It is also a grantee agency of the Economic Opportunity Program.

Accomplishments. Through its involvement with the Chemung County Child Care Council, the program shares staff and parent training with other child-care programs and jointly advocates on behalf of children's needs. With the public schools, the program operates a preschool program featuring joint intake procedures, family assessments, and referrals. The program, which provides parent education, shares school space, and schools provide busing for the children. The program has developed an Early Childhood Center, which houses the Association for Retarded Citizens, United Cerebral Palsy, Head Start, and the Elmira Psychiatric Center Preschool Program, and fosters coordination of services, staff sharing, and a joint intake committee for collaborative planning, assessment, and placement of children.

NEW YORK STATE CHILD CARE COORDINATING COUNCIL
237 Bradford St., Albany, NY 12206
Sandra Lamm/Louise Stoney   (518) 463-8663

Goals/Objectives. The council seeks to increase the amount of affordable, quality child care through direct services to parents and providers and through advocacy.

History. Created as the Child Care Council in 1975, this organization began as a support group for the state R&Rs. In 1985, increased funding allowed permanent staff to be hired and the scope of the agency's work to be expanded.

Membership/Structure. Membership includes three categories: affiliates (typically one per county, usually the R&R), organizational members, and individual members. Monthly meetings of both the membership and the board are held. The membership includes active committees on child-care legislation, child-care regulations, provider training, data collection, welfare reform, collaboration/coordination, CDA scholarships, and others as needed.

Accomplishments. Through the Advocacy and Education Project, the council has (1) brought together the PreK Directors Association, the Head Start Association, and day-care providers to create recommendations to the legislature on coordination of services; (2) addressed welfare reform by making recommendations to the legislature on coordination of and access to services under the Family Support Act (FSA); (3) reviewed and commented on state child-care regulations; (4) successfully advocated for state salary grants to augment provider salaries under subsidized day care; (5) advocated that reimbursement rates be increased; and (6) created a directory for providers, policy makers, and the public of day-care licensing and funding agencies. The Data Collection Project has issued a manual and trained R&Rs on a common computer system, by means of which it is compiling statewide data on child-care supply and demand.

North Carolina

FAMILY SERVICE CENTERS (STATE)

Department of Public Instruction, Education Building, Room 322, Raleigh, NC 27603-1712

Laura Mast   (919) 733-8307

Goals/Objectives.   A State Early Childhood Task Force was formed to develop a state model for school-based programs for 3- and 4-year-olds and their families.

History.   The task force was convened in 1988; out of their deliberations and recommendations grew the concept of Family Service Centers, programs that would assess community needs and address them using an interagency approach. Eight model programs are currently operating.

Membership/Structure.   The task force is made up of Department of Public Instruction staff, school superintendents, public school teachers, pre-school and day-care teachers, university educators, and parents. Informally, individuals from a foundation and private industry also participate. The group meets as needed to address problems perceived in the state's early childhood education system. Between meetings, members often communicate informally.

Accomplishments.   The task force recommendations have been implemented through eight Family Service Centers. Each center is required to do a community needs assessment and then to meet these needs through inter-agency efforts, which may include collaboration with health professionals to provide preventive and primary care, collaboration with the state employment security agency to provide training and employment assistance, collaboration with community colleges to provide adult literacy, parenting, and general education, collaboration with schools to provide developmentally appropriate programs and transitions between center child-care programs and kindergarten, and collaboration with Head Start to share staff training and consultant services.

Ohio

CHILD DAY CARE PLANNING PROJECT

614 Superior Ave. N.W., Suite 300, Cleveland, OH 44113-1306

Carole Ellison   (216) 781-2944

Goals/Objectives.   The project was formed to address issues in the child-care delivery system, such as quality, access, and cost.

History.   The project was initiated by a 1982 day-care needs assessment collaboratively performed by the United Way Services, the County Department of Human Services, and the Federation for Community Planning. In 1984 demonstration and research efforts were initiated, and in 1988 services were institutionalized. After the project ended in July 1990, successful initiatives were continued by a comprehensive resource and referral center.

Membership/Structure.   The project is governed by a committee representing the United Way Services, the Department of Human Services, the Federation for Community Planning, Head Start, city officials, community and private foundations, federated charities, and other community groups.

Accomplishments. The project's activities include the following: (1) demonstration school-aged child-care programs; (2) funding for integrating elders with a center-based child-care program; (3) training for day-care providers, including collaboration with a community college infant-toddler model program and day-care provider scholarships; (4) financial assistance to parents through child-care scholarships; (5) a capital loan program to assist day-care facilities with refurbishment and capital improvements and to provide day-care homes with equipment; (6) maintaining a database on child-care needs and resources; (7) funding centers to sponsor networks of family day-care homes; and (8) bringing funders together to develop better funding policies.

FAMILY LIFE PROGRAM
Department of Education, 65 South Front St., Room 912, Columbus, OH 43266-0308
Linda Reece   (614) 466-3046

Goals/Objectives. The program strengthens families by enhancing adults' life skills, offering parenting education, and making referrals to other services.

History. Begun originally in 1939 with federal funds, the program expanded its goals and changed its structure over the years. With the advent of state funds in 1985, the program was opened to families of all income levels and developed an interdepartmental advisory committee to oversee the program.

Membership/Structure. The program's state supervisor serves on advisory committees representing the Departments of Education, Health, Human Services, Economic Development, and Mental Health and Mental Retardation. Local programs are also advised by collaborative committees, and state-local meetings are held three times a year.

Accomplishments. Local programs provide on-site child care while parents receive instruction and counseling. University research indicates that participants in the program develop more effective parenting skills. Programs are located in extremely depressed areas, providing access to the most disadvantaged families. Locally, Head Start and family life programs share training, make mutual referrals, and plan transitions; many children are dual enrolled. At the state level, agencies represented on the advisory committee share data on services and participate in collaborative program planning.

GRADUATION, REALITY AND DUAL ROLE SKILLS (GRADS)
Department of Education, 65 South Front St., Room 912, Columbus, OH 43266-0308
Gene Todd   (614) 466-3046

Goals/Objectives. The program's objectives are (1) to increase the likelihood that participants will remain in school during pregnancy and after the birth of their child, and stay to the point of graduation; (2) to help participants carry out positive health care practices for themselves and their children in both prenatal and postnatal stages; (3) to provide participants with knowledge and skills related to child development and positive parenting practices; (4) to prepare participants for the world of work; and (5) to encourage participants to set goals toward balancing work and family.

History. GRADS began in 1980 in response to the state's high school dropout rate.

Membership/Structure. At the state level, informal collaborative relationships exist with the Single Homemaker Grant Committee, which awards funds to GRADS participants for their child-care and transportation needs, and with the Perinatal Regional Network, in its health education initiatives. Locally, GRADS programs network with community agencies, hospitals, and schools to facilitate access for participants, and each local program is supervised by an interagency advisory committee.

Accomplishments. Since the program's implementation, the dropout rate has varied between 5.2% and 16%, much lower than the national average. Participants have healthier babies with higher birth weights. Through participation in parenting training, participants score higher on tests on appropriate developmental and behavioral expectations of children and nonviolent approaches to behavior management. GRADS is an exemplary program recognized by the U.S. Department of Education as a National Diffusion Network program to be disseminated throughout the United States.

INTERAGENCY EMPLOYEES CORPORATION
17273 State Rte. 104, Chillicothe, OH 45601
Jim Lambert   (614) 775-1432

Goals/Objectives. The collaboration's mission is to become a rural institutional model for child care. The objectives are to provide an extended latchkey program for kindergarten through grade 6 pupils, a preschool program, and an infant-toddler program.

History. The nonprofit corporation was founded in 1987 by employees of the Veterans Administration Medical Center, two state of Ohio correctional institutions, and the local schools, after a need for a child-care facility for their employees and the local community was established.

Membership/Structure. A 15-member volunteer board of directors meets monthly. The chairman of the board serves a 3-year term; other board members rotate every 3 years as well. The program director and co-director have formal training and degrees in elementary education and business administration, respectively. Representation on the board is based on the size of the member organizations. Decisions are made by a majority vote. A staff of 14, many of whom are college students, run programs.

Accomplishments. The collaboration has (1) published a "how-to" book on organizing collaborative efforts as well as sponsored two national conferences on the "how-to's"; (2) published a parents's handbook on quality child care; (3) provided transportation covering a major part of the county area; (4) provided tuition assistance from Title XX and other sources and established a policy opening the center to the public; (5) established a smoothly functioning collaborative process among federal, state, and local agencies; (6) published an employee's handbook; (7) routinely sponsored child-care worker certification and continuing education workshops for surrounding communities; and (8) consulted with other agencies and communities on child-care issues.

LOOKING AT LIFE THROUGH LITERACY PROGRAM
Council of Economic Opportunities, 668 Euclid Ave. #700, Cleveland, O H 44114
Dorothy Cheeks   (216) 696-9077

Goals/Objectives.   The program was established to enhance the ability of parents of Head Start children to identify and set life goals aimed at improving their economic self-sufficiency by helping them determine their interests and abilities and learn life and literacy skills.

History.   Piloted in 1987 by the council with federal funds, the program involved participants from seven Head Start delegate agencies. A Case Western Reserve University evaluation of the program indicated its success, and it has been implemented throughout the council's Head Start agencies. The program has received regional and national attention.

Membership/Structure.   The program is taught by Head Start staff; professionals from the community teach in their areas of expertise; staff of the Food and Nutrition Education Program of the Department of Agriculture teach topics on health and nutrition; community groups, such as health clinics, libraries, and social service agencies, organize visits for participants; and participants shadow professionals in their fields of interest at their worksites.

Accomplishments.   The Case Western Reserve University evaluation indicated positive change in participants in the areas of knowledge of community resources, indication of job or career plans, identification of a self-improvement goal, skills for living, and knowledge of and access to skills necessary for making changes. Participants report higher-quality family relationships and demonstrate greater interest in their children's education, both at Head Start and later, when they go to school. Participants demonstrate greater self-sufficiency in accessing community resources, develop oral and written communication skills, and acquire employment as a result of the program.

Oregon

OREGON CHILDREN AND YOUTH SERVICES COMMISSION
530 Center St. N.E., Suite 300, Salem, OR 97310
Vickie Stott   (503) 373-1283

Goals/Objectives.   The commission (1) administers grants for children's programs; (2) based on local input, develops and recommends state policy on services to children and families; (3) fosters comprehensive planning at local and state levels for services to children up to the age of 18; and (4) encourages local and state coordination services.

History. In 1989, as a result of the findings of the 1988 Governor's Children's Agenda, the commission was formed as a planning and coordination vehicle for children's programs, superseding committees and programs previously established.

Membership/Structure. The commission is appointed by the governor and represents schools, child care, Head Start, health, mental health, the courts, and business. The commission meets monthly, and subcommittees meet in between. Six regional coordinators assist with local planning and grant applications and serve as liaisons between the commission and local commissions.

Accomplishments. The commission has established 36 county children and youth services commissions that collaboratively assess and plan for community needs. The commission provides technical assistance and responds to the findings of these local commissions by recommending state policy. Through its grants, the commission supports Great Start programs for children up to age 6. Based on community planning and coordination, local commissions administer Great Start funds to promote child care and child development, promote health and mental health, provide parent education and support, and improve access to services.

OREGON PREKINDERGARTEN PROGRAM

Department of Education, 700 Pringle Pkwy. S.E., Salem, OR 97310
Randy Hitz   (503) 378-5585

Goals/Objectives. The collaboration awards grants to local collaborative initiatives to increase services to needy children and to foster state-local collaboration in program planning.

History. In 1986, the Oregon Department of Education received a federal technical assistance grant to create a State Early Childhood Initiatives Project, which assessed early childhood education in the state and identified gaps and deficiencies in services. In 1987, legislation was passed to meet the identified needs, resulting in the creation of the prekindergarten program in 1988.

Membership/Structure. The program is housed under the auspices of the Department of Education and is collaboratively administered by an advisory committee representing mental health, welfare, the public schools, the legislature, the governor's office, community colleges, and Head Start. Members are appointed by the superintendent of schools and the commissioner of community colleges, and they meet quarterly.

Accomplishments. The program has stimulated collaborative local program planning by funding joint initiatives among such agencies as Head Start, the public schools, and social service agencies. The program provides technical assistance to communities in establishing collaborative programs and planning groups. It has stimulated growth in services to children by funding initiatives in areas previously unserved by any early childhood program, awarding expansion grants to existing programs. Local prekindergarten programs encourage parent involvement, meet Head Start performance standards for education and social services, and provide experiences for children that are coordinated and consistent with public school programs.

Pennsylvania

DELAWARE VALLEY CHILD CARE COUNCIL
401 North Broad St., Suite 1818, Philadelphia, PA 19108
Letty Thall   (215) 922-7526

Goals/Objectives. The council's goal is to promote the development of a regional child day-care delivery system that ensures accessible, quality child-care services.

History. The council was formed as a result of a United Way–funded report on child care issues in the Delaware Valley, conducted by a 50-member study group representing the Department of Public Welfare, business, child care, county governments, and community groups. In 1985, as a result of the recommendations of the study group, the council was formed with a corporate grant.

Membership/Structure. Staff of the council support the initiatives of its working board of directors, whose members represent the Departments of Education and Public Welfare, private industry, child-care providers, early childhood and child-care professional organizations, higher education, parents, the public schools, labor and community groups, and city and county governments.

Accomplishments. The council has developed and implemented a Shared Substitute Program, for which it recruits day-care providers and sends them as needed to area centers and homes. This program has created a pool of qualified applicants from which child-care programs can hire new employees. The council offers technical assistance to day-care providers, community groups, and schools starting school-aged child-care programs and has developed a report for home providers explaining zoning laws and how to comply with them. The council successfully advocated for Title XX subsidy increases of $3.7 million in fiscal year 1989 and has written a cost-sharing plan and a child-care professional wage policy brochure that describe how parents, the private sector, and the government can share day-care costs while enhancing provider benefits. The council has also produced a six-volume child-care needs assessment.

FARRELL AREA SCHOOL DISTRICT CHILD CARE
Early Intervention Program, Roemer Blvd., Farrell, PA 16121
Sandy Joseph   (412) 346-6585

Goals/Objectives. The program's broad goal is to enhance the quality of services to young children. Long-term goals include: (1) developing an intergenerational component to the program; (2) linking more frequently with the business community; and (3) acquiring additional space for an early childhood center.

History. The program began 15 years ago as a means to share resources in order to provide comprehensive services to youngsters. Over the years, the structure of the collaborative relationships has responded to the changing needs of the community.

Membership/Structure. Originally established as a preschool council, collaborative relationships have broadened to include collaborative preschool screening with area day-care providers, subcontracts to center-based day-care providers to care for children referred by the program, a network of family day-care homes affiliated with the program, a joint teen-parent program and a center-based infant-toddler program with another school district, a consortium of child-care agencies, and the designation of the school district as the single point of contact for Department of Public Assistance clients.

Accomplishments. Head Start, child care, and special needs services are fully integrated. Teachers receive joint training and are compensated equitably. R&R is provided to parents, with both referral and placement services offered. Transitions are planned between programs, and team teaching with special education teachers accommodates the needs of handicapped youngsters in mainstream settings. Parents participate in Head Start parenting education; all participants are on a common database; programs are guided by common regulations, share resources, jointly purchase materials, plan programs collaboratively, and share a common curriculum.

ADVISOR TO THE GOVERNOR ON CHILD CARE POLICY

Governor's Office of Policy Development, Room 506, Finance Building, Harrisburg, PA 17120
Elizabeth Milder Beh   (717) 787-8595

Goals/Objectives. The council was established to recommend a comprehensive agenda of children's policies (birth through age 6) to the governor.

History. Established by executive order in September 1989, the Governor's Advisory Council for Young Children builds on the Governor's Child Care Initiative, which (1) created child-care models for government employees, (2) involved schools in child care, (3) coordinated the cabinet agencies to advise on child care, and (4) worked to develop comprehensive policies for child care and education.

Membership/Structure. The governor is chairperson. The governor's advisor on child-care policy is vice-chairperson. Staff is composed of the chief of staff (a visiting professor from Penn State) and policy analysts from the governor's policy office. Membership represents labor, business, government, higher education, child-care advocates, Head Start, schools, and parents. Members meet every 2 months and communicate informally between meetings.

Accomplishments. The council's accomplishments include the following: (1) facilitated community assessments of conditions for children and (2) completed a policy report for the Governor, *Community for Families, Families for Children: Directions for Holistic Policy Development in Pennsylvania.* The report was presented to the governor in November 1990.

PENNSYLVANIA ASSOCIATION FOR THE EDUCATION OF YOUNG CHILDREN
1060 Morewood Ave., Pittsburgh, PA 15213
Marsha Poster   (412) 687-6394

Goals/Objectives. The group's goal is to serve as a conduit for information about early childhood education and related services for young children and to advocate on children's issues with other early childhood groups.

History. The group was established as an affiliate of the National Association for the Education of Young Children.

Membership/Structure. The group meets four times yearly, convened by its president. A board of directors made up of the AEYC's membership meets before or after each full meeting and maintains frequent phone contact.

Accomplishments. The group's activities include: (1) statewide dissemination of a newsletter listing early childhood job openings and training opportunities; (2) representation on the Governor's Advisory Council on Young Children and creation of a State Task Force on Child Care in the Public Schools; (3) creation of "Questions to the Candidates" on child-care issues, given to candidates for the state legislature (their answers are disseminated to the public); (4) with the Department of Education, development of an early childhood accreditation policy, with recommendations to the legislature; (5) publication, with the Delaware Valley Child Care Council, of a brochure on child-care costs and provider wages; and (6) testimony against new Department of Public Welfare licensing regulations, resulting in revisions by the department with input from the AEYC.

Rhode Island

INTEGRATION OF SPECIAL NEEDS INFANTS/TODDLERS INTO COMMUNITY BASED PROGRAMS
Handicapped Children's Early Education Demonstration Project, Department of Special Education, Rhode Island College, Providence, RI 02908
Thomas T. Kochanek, Ph.D.   (401) 456-8599

Goals/Objectives. The primary objective of this project is to develop formal affiliations between early intervention program and day-care providers such that special needs infants/toddlers receive their recommended "intervention" within existing day care settings.

History. The integrated group project was developed to create community-based, integrated service options for disabled and vulnerable children and their families enrolled in early intervention programs.

Membership/Structure. The project serves children and families within two regions of the state and is affiliated with 25 day-care facilities and family day-care homes. Each site is advised by a policy committee, which includes parents, early intervention staff, and day-care staff.

Accomplishments. Approximately 100 children have participated in this project, and evaluation data reflect several positive outcomes. From the parents' perspective, the primary benefits reported include:

- the opportunity for special needs children to interact with age appropriate peers
- the promotion of acceptance of special needs children and their families in the overall community
- the information provided to families about normal growth and development
- the opportunity for families to increase their friendships and social support network

With regard to the day-care provider's perspective, major assets of this program include:

- assistance to day-care staff in acquiring skills and understandings that benefit both special needs and non-special-needs children
- provision to day-care staff with support and resources that reduce isolation and increase their professional identity, growth, and development
- tremendous growth for special needs children, particularly in the areas of language and social/emotional competence

PUBLIC POLICY COALITION FOR RHODE ISLAND CHILDREN
485 Mt. Pleasant Ave., Providence, RI 02908
Alexandra Moser and Maryann Finamore   (401) 274-3094

Goals/Objectives. The coalition's objectives are to advocate on child-care issues on the state level and to increase community awareness, thereby creating broad-based support for child-care issues.

History. The collaboration grew out of discussions between the president of the Rhode Island Association for the Education of Young Children and the chair of the Rhode Island Daycare Directors Association about the need for change in early care and education in the state. The goals and objectives were set in 1985, when several nonprofit organizations—including child-care groups, Head Start, the schools, and social service agencies—joined together.

Membership/Structure. All members are volunteers pledged to serve a 2-year term. Monthly meetings are held, and a very strong support system is used on a daily basis through phone contact. A committee structure is used for such purposes as developing legislation.

Accomplishments. As a result of the coalition (1) AFDC families now have the option of both low-income sliding scale and 4A disregard of welfare;

(2) 1989 legislation has established a permanent commission on child care; (3) legislation has been passed providing state funds to schools to transport children to day care; (4) income eligibility guidelines have been raised from 165 percent to 185 percent of the poverty line; and (5) legislation has been passed to allow up to $30,000 in tax credits for employers who provide on-site child care.

Texas

HOGG FOUNDATION FOR MENTAL HEALTH
University of Texas, Austin, TX 78713
Louise Iscoe (512) 471-5041

Goals/Objectives. The group's objective is to promote mental health among the people of Texas.

History. The agency was established in 1940 by funds bequeathed by Will Hogg to the University of Texas for improvement of the lives of the people of Texas. His sister, Ima Hogg, defined mental health as the field for action and, in 1964, created the Ima Hogg Foundation solely to serve Houston residents. Concern about child-care issues has arisen recently because of the impact on family mental health when child care is not affordable or accessible, especially for special needs children.

Membership/Structure. The foundation is an endowment within the University of Texas and the university's board of regents serves as board of directors. The agency is served by an executive committee, representing agency staff and university faculty, and by a national advisory council of health experts. A faculty advisory committee provides technical assistance and consultation to the programs funded by the agency. Commissions address community care of the mentally ill, the mental health of adolescents and young adults, and the mental health of children and their families.

Accomplishments. The agency (1) conducts outreach to other foundations, agencies, and individuals to foster joint seminars and conferences and cooperative funding of large-scale projects; (2) has fostered the development of a School-of-Tomorrow Program involving preschool, elementary, and early secondary education by major grants to support four programs for 5 years and by encouraging interagency collaboration among school and health and human service agencies; (3) funds and provides technical assistance to programs in Texas addressing the needs of young children and their families; and (4) encourages collaboration through public newsletters and publications, including reports on the status of child care in the state and a "how-to" manual for developing collaborations.

DAY CARE ASSOCIATION OF FORT WORTH AND TARRANT COUNTY
P.O. Box 7935, Fort Worth, TX 76111
John Widner (817) 831-0374

Goals/Objectives. The agency's objectives are to provide child-care services and increase the supply of child-care services to families of all income levels.

History. The agency was established in 1968 as a result of a community study that recommended a merger of three child-care agencies in Fort Worth, expansion of services, and improvement of the quality of service. The merger would result in a better working relationship between service sites to better serve children and families. Since that time, the agency has grown to serve approximately 3,000 children in a system comprised of day-care centers, Head Start centers, family day-care homes, a broker system, and a corporate child-care program.

Membership/Structure. The agency is a nonprofit corporation with a board of directors setting policy and a professional managing executive director. There are three advisory councils that relate to specific programs. These are the Welfare Reform Program, Head Start, and the Comprehensive Child Development Program.

Accomplishments. The agency has increased the availability of child-care services in several ways. The following listing depicts these expanded services.

1. Merged significant child-care program under one coordinated umbrella. This includes:
   a. Establishment and expansion of Head Start to 14 centers
   b. Establishment and operation of a city-funded program that operates two centers
   c. Establishment and operation of a corporate child-care center in conjunction with the Tandy Corporation
   d. Establishment and operation of a handicapped consortium for north Texas area for handicapped children
   e. Establishment and operation of a broker program utilizing nonagency centers and day homes
2. Has developed proposals and been funded for the following new programs or service delivery methods:
   a. Comprehensive Child Development Program funded by ACYF as a study of early intervention effects on families and children. This project, which is one of 22 in the nation, consists of two Child Development Centers serving 120 focus children plus their siblings, as well as a case management component for family support
   b. Selection as one of four field test sites for a Welfare Reform Child Care Management Service for Tarrant County; it will serve as a prototype for the rest of the state
   c. Awarded a contract for Welfare Reform Child Care Management Service for north Texas, composed of 13 counties. In the Welfare Reform Child Care Management Service, the agency coordinates community resources for service, determines eligibility, provides centralized information for parents, facilitates the enrollment of children and funds, and

monitors all child-care programs supported by the Welfare Reform Program, which utilizes Title XX and other federal monies.

In addition, the agency has opened and administered new day-care centers in cooperation with a church and with a low-income housing development authority.

Virginia

COUNCIL ON CHILD DAY CARE AND EARLY CHILDHOOD PROGRAMS

Washington Bldg., Suite 1116, 1100 Bank St., Richmond, VA 23219
Linda Sawyers   (804) 371-8603

Goals/Objectives. The council was established to (1) promote quality early childhood programs for at-risk children; (2) increase affordability and access across the state; and (3) foster public- and private-sector collaboration. The council is also responsible for the development of a biennial state plan for child care and early education.

History. Several state levels and legislative study committees recommended the formation of the council, which was formally endorsed and mandated by state legislation in 1989.

Membership/Structure. The council's members are appointed by the governor and represent parents, the business sector, child care, and Head Start. Staff support the council's initiatives, and the council meets quarterly.

Accomplishments. The council has garnered $1 million in state funds to support a series of demonstration and planning projects statewide to increase availability and service delivery. Demonstration projects must involve parents and indicate local collaboration and coordination of services; planning grants are for communities with limited child care to do a local needs and resources assessment and develop a local child-care plan. The council has received a 3-year Head Start Collaboration Grant from the Federal Administration for Children, Youth and Families, Head Start Bureau, to provide for state-level collaboration of Head Start and to expand Head Start to every county in the state. In addition, the council has been designated by the governor as the lead agency to administer the new Child Care and Development Block Grant, which will bring about $13.5 million into the state.

Washington

EARLY CHILDHOOD EDUCATION AND ASSISTANCE PROGRAM

Department of Community Development, 9th St. and Columbia Bldg., MS/GH-51, Olympia, WA 98504
Mary Frost   (206) 753-4106

Goals/Objectives. The program's objectives are to (1) build a child-focused program that includes the entire family and addresses empowerment for parents, service providers, and local communities; and (2) encourage collaboration in delivering services.

History. In 1985, the program was started by state legislation growing out of the Governor's Agenda for Education. The program is the cornerstone of the state's educational efforts and has bipartisan support.

Membership/Structure. The program is administered by the Department of Community Development, whose director is appointed by the governor, and the staff supports the initiatives of an interagency advisory committee representing children's advocates, higher education, public schools, and Head Start. Subcommittees address particular issues. Additionally, the staff collaborates with the Business Roundtable, a CEO group.

Accomplishments. Local programs are administered by a variety of agencies, including community colleges, child-care agencies, Head Start, schools, social service agencies, and county and city governments. All programs provide comprehensive services through collaboration with other agencies, such as coordinating transportation, sharing staff training, planning transitions to kindergarten, conducting collaborative needs assessments, and participating in collaborative community planning. At the state level, the program co-sponsors training conferences with the Washington AEYC and advocacy groups and participates in a collaborative effort to revise child-care regulations to create comparability among Head Start, special education, and child-care services.

Wisconsin

EARLY DEVELOPMENT AWARENESS PROJECT
Donges Bay Elementary School, 2401 West Donges Bay Rd., Mequon, WI 53092
Leesa Maxwell   (414) 242-4260

Goals/Objectives. The project seeks to conduct and facilitate appropriate developmental screening of young children; provide screening training to preschool staff; identify community resources that provide child development information and services to parents of young children; facilitate cooperative efforts between resource agencies and people; and provide and coordinate developmental information services.

History. The project was established in 1986 by the school district to improve the number of appropriate early referrals of children for special education services.

Membership/Structure. Staff of the program network with preschool and day-care staff, private schools, parents, and community groups to foster appropriate referrals of children and coordination of community resources.

Accomplishments. For parents, the program has provided information services in collaboration with public health nurses, the Ozaukee County extension home economist, Milwaukee Area Technical College, and Family Services of Mequon-Thiensville; displayed developmental information posters at community locations; initiated a newsletter; provided referrals and follow-up to needed services; organized parent education and support groups; and published a listing and description of local day-care and preschool services. The program has improved the number of appropriate, early referrals of children for special education services by increasing communication between pediatricians, day-care providers, and parents; developing a training module for providers on detection and screening of developmental delays; discussing developmental delays with parents; and referring children to Child Find. This training qualifies for Wisconsin Department of Public Instruction continuing education units and for day-care licensing inservice credits. It has been disseminated statewide. The training document and videotape are available for purchase.

FAMILY AND CHILD LEARNING CENTERS OF N.E.W., INC.
1201 Main St., P.O. Box 44, Oconto, WI 54153
Lauretta Willette   (414) 834-2877

Goals/Objectives. The agency serves low-income preschool children and their families by providing opportunities to develop family self-sufficiency.

History. A Head Start grantee since 1965, the agency became involved in collaborative relationships starting in 1980, when it established an interagency agreement with the school district to serve handicapped preschool children.

Membership/Structure. The agency has developed collaborative relationships with schools, universities, and health and social service organizations. Interagency meetings are held to oversee collaborative programs.

Accomplishments. Through collaboration, the agency provides comprehensive services to children in the areas of health, speech and language therapy, and cultural activities. Parents receive training through the county extension service and health and family-planning assistance through a local family-planning clinic. Staff receives cross-agency training. The agency participates in joint community needs assessments with the county extension service and provides technical assistance and training to child-care programs in the area. In addition, the agency has just entered into a collaborative effort with an area college to participate in the establishment of an intergenerational facility on campus. The agency's program will be housed in a college building and will provide Head Start, day care, and adult day care. This new program will link senior adults to Head Start children, place student teachers in the classroom, and share adult and staff training.

References

Administration for Children, Youth and Families. (1990). *Child care coordination: Information memorandum for all Head Start grantees and delegate agencies.* Washington, DC: U.S. Department of Health and Human Services (ACYF-IM-90-02).

Allington, R. L., & Johnston, P. (1989). Coordination, collaboration and consistency: The redesign of compensatory and special education interventions. In R. E. Slavin, N. L. Karweit, & N. A. Madden (Eds.), *Effective programs for students at risk* (pp. 320–354). Boston: Allyn & Bacon.

American Institutes for Research in the Behavioral Sciences. (1980). *Project Connections: A study of child care information and referral services.* Cambridge, MA: Author.

American Psychological Association. (1988). *Thesaurus of psychological index terms* (5th ed.). Washington, DC: Author.

Anthony, R. N., & Young, D. W. (1984). *Management control in nonprofit organizations.* Homewood, IL: Irwin.

Appley, D. G., & Winder, A. E. (1977a). An evolving definition of collaboration and some implications for the world of work. *The Journal of Applied Behavioral Science, 13*(3), 279–291.

Appley, D. G., & Winder, A. E. (1977b). Introduction [to Special issue]. *The Journal of Applied Behavioral Science, 13*(3), 264–267.

Bass, G. (1983, March). Social shock: The devolution of human services. In *Perspectives on interagency collaboration.* National Invitational Symposium on Interagency Collaboration, Denver, CO. (ERIC Document Reproduction Service No. 235 669)

Beatty, B. R. (1981). *A vocation from on high: Preschool advocacy and teaching as an occupation for women in nineteenth-century Boston.* Unpublished doctoral dissertation, Harvard Graduate School of Education. (Cited in Cahan)

Beck, R. (1982). Beyond the stalemate in child care public policy. In E. Zigler & E. Gordon (Eds.), *Day care: Scientific and social policy issues* (pp. 307–337). Boston: Auburn House.

Benard, B. (1989). Working together: Principles of effective collaboration. *Prevention Forum, 10*(1), 4–9.

Bennis, W. G. (1966). *Changing organizations: Essays on the development and evolution of human organization.* New York: McGraw-Hill.

Berkowitz, J. S. (1986, October-November). Extending the collaborative spirit at the Philadelphia Museum of Art. *Museum News,* pp. 28–35.

Berrueta-Clement, J. R., Schweinhart, L. J., Barnett, W. S., Epstein, A. S., &

Weikart, D. P. (1984). *Changed lives: The effects of the Perry Preschool Program on youths through age 19*. Ypsilanti, MI: High/Scope.

Billingsley, A., & Giovannoni, J. M. (1972). *Children of the storm: Black children and American child welfare*. New York: Harcourt Brace Jovanovich.

Black, B. J., & Kase, H. M. (1963). Interagency cooperation in rehabilitation and mental health. *Social Service Review, 37*(1), 26–32.

Bredekamp, S. (Ed.). (1987). *Developmentally appropriate practice in early childhood programs serving children from birth through age 8*. Washington, DC: National Association for the Education of Young Children.

Bremner, R. H. (1970–1974). *Children and youth in America* (Vol. 2, pts. 1–6). Cambridge, MA: Harvard University Press.

Brewer, G. D., & deLeon, P. (1983). *The foundations of policy analysis*. Chicago: Dorsey.

Brewer, G. D., & Kakalik, J. S. (1979). *Handicapped children: Strategies for improving services*. New York: McGraw-Hill.

Bronfenbrenner, U. (1979). *The ecology of human development: Experiments by nature and design*. Cambridge, MA: Harvard University Press.

Bruner, C. (1989). *Is change from above possible? State-level strategies for supporting street-level services*. Paper presented at the Association for Public Policy Analysis and Management, Alexandria, VA.

Bruner, C. (1991). *Thinking collaboratively: Ten question and answers to help policy makers improve children's services*. Washington, DC: Education and Human Services Consortium.

Burgard, R. (1983, August). Cultural cooperation: The new frontier. *Museum News*, pp. 20–29.

Cahan, E. (1989). *Past caring*. New York: National Center for Children in Poverty, School of Public Health, Columbia University.

Caldwell, B. (1986). Day care and the public schools: Natural allies, natural enemies. *Educational Leadership, 43*(5), 34–39.

Carew, D. K. (1976). *Some necessary values: Toward collaborative organizations*. Unpublished manuscript, University of Massachusetts.

Caruso, J. (1981, April). Collaboration of school, college and community: A bridge to progress. *Educational Leadership, 38*, 558–562.

CCI&R Issues. (1983–1986). [Newsletter; see especially *1* (1–5), *2* (2–4), *3* (1)]. (Available from National Association of Child Care Resource and Referral Agencies, 2116 Campus Dr. SE, Rochester, MN 55904)

Chapel Hill Training Outreach Project. (1988). *Transitions from pre-school to kindergarten*. Chapel Hill, NC: Author.

Clarke-Stewart, K. A. (1977). *Child care in the family*. New York: Academic Press.

Cohen, D. L. (1989, March 15). Collaboration: What works. *Education Week*, p. 13.

Committee for Economic Development. (1987). *Children in need: Investment strategies for the educationally disadvantaged*. New York: Author.

Congressional Budget Office. (1978). *Child care and preschool: Options for federal support*. Washington, DC: U.S. Government Printing Office.

Council of Chief State School Officers. (1989). *Success for all in a new century*. Washington, DC: Author.

Covey, J. G., & Brown, L. D. (1985). *Beyond strategic planning: Strategic decisions in nonprofit organization*. Boston: Institute for Development Research.

Cummings, T. G., & Huse, E. F. (1989). *Organizational development and change* (4th ed.). St. Paul, MN: West.

Davidson, S. M. (1976). Planning and coordination of social services in multiorganizational contexts. *Social Science Review, 51*, 117–137.

De Bevoise, W. (1986). Collaboration: Some principles of bridgework. *Educational Leadership, 43*(5), 9–12.

Derlega, V. J., & Grzelak, J. (Eds.). (1982). *Cooperation and helping behavior: Theories and research*. New York: Academic Press.

Drummond, W., & Baker, M. D. (1974). *A state of the art paper re research on collaboration in teacher education* (Final Report). Tallahassee, FL: Florida State Department of Education.

Dunkle, M., & Nash, M. (1989). Creating effective interagency collaboratives. *Education Week, 8*(25), 44.

Edgar, E., & Maddox, M. (1983, March). The cookbook model: An approach to interagency collaboration. In *Perspectives on interagency collaboration*. National Invitational Symposium on Interagency Collaboration, Denver, CO. (ERIC Document Reproduction Service No. ED 235 669)

Elder, J. O., & Magrab, P. R. (1980). *Coordinating services to handicapped children: A handbook for interagency collaboration*. Baltimore: Brookes.

Ellwood, D. T. (1988). *Poor support: Poverty in the American family*. New York: Basic Books.

Emery, F. E., & Trist, E. L. (1973). *Towards a social ecology*. New York: Plenum.

Etzioni, A. (1964). *Modern organizations*. Englewood Cliffs, NJ: Prentice-Hall.

Euben, D., & Reisman, B. (1990). *Making the connections: Public-private partnerships in child care*. New York: Child Care Action Campaign.

Fein, G., & Clarke-Stewart, A. (1973). *Day care in context*. New York: Wiley.

Fletcher, R., & Cole, J. T. (1988). *Interagency collaboration among rural special education programs: How is it done and is it working?* Las Cruces, NM: New Mexico State University, New Mexico Department of Education. (ERIC Document Reproduction Service No. ED 299 751)

Flynn, C. C., & Harbin, G. L. (1987). Evaluating interagency coordination efforts using a multidimensional interactional, developmental paradigm. *Remedial and Special Education, 8*(3), 35–44.

Fombrun, C. J. (1986). Structural dynamics within and between organizations. *Administrative Science Quarterly, 31*, 403–421.

Fox, M. F., & Faver, C. A. (1984). Independence and cooperation in research: The motivations and costs of collaboration. *Journal of Higher Education, 55*(3), 347–359.

Fuhrman, S. H., & Elmore, R. F. (1990). Understanding local control in the wake of state education reform. *Educational Evaluation and Policy Analysis, 12*(1), 82–96.

Fulghum, R. (1990). *All I really need to know I learned in kindergarten: Uncommon thoughts on common things.* New York: Villard.

Gage, R. W. (1976). Integration of human services delivery systems. *Public Welfare, 34*(1), 27–32.

Galaskiewicz, J., & Shatin, D. (1981). Leadership and networking among neighborhood human service organization. *Administrative Science Quarterly, 26,* 434–448.

Gallagher, J. J., Harbin, G., Thomas, D., Clifford, R., & Wenger, M. (1988). *Major policy issues in implementing Part H—P.L. 99-457 (infants and toddlers).* Chapel Hill: University of North Carolina at Chapel Hill, Carolina Institute for Child and Family Policy.

Gamm, L. (1981). An introduction to research in interorganizational relations (IOR). *Journal of Voluntary Action Research, 10*(3–4), 18–52.

Gamm, L. D. (1983). Interorganizational relations and the management of voluntary health organizations. In M. S. Moyer (Ed.), *Managing voluntary organizations: Proceedings of a conference held at York University* (pp. 25–43). Toronto, Canada.

Gans, S. P., & Horton, G. T. (1975). *Integration of human services: The state and municipal levels.* New York: Praeger.

Gardner, S. (1990). Failure by fragmentation. *Equity and Choice, 6*(2), 4–12.

Garwood, S., Fewell, R., & Neisworth, J. (1988). Public law 99-457: You can get from there to here. *Topics in Early Childhood Special Education, 8,* 1–11.

Golden, O. (1988, October). *Balancing entrepreneurship, line worker discretion and political accountability: The delicate task of innovators in human services.* Paper presented at the annual meeting of the Association for Public Policy Analysis and Management, Seattle, WA.

Golden, O. (1989). *Innovation in public sector human service programs: The implications of innovation by "groping along."* Unpublished manuscript.

Golden, O., Skinner, M., & Baker, R. (1990). *Welfare reform and poor children: Collaboration and case management approaches.* Unpublished manuscript.

Goldring, M. (1986, October-November). Getting together: Costs and benefits of a consortium. *Museum News,* pp. 36–41.

Goodman, I. F., & Brady, J. P. (1988). *The challenge of coordination: Head Start's relationship to state-funded preschool initiatives.* Newton, MA: Educational Development Center.

Gray, B. (1985). Conditions facilitating interorganizational collaboration. *Human Relations, 38*(10), 911–936.

Gray, B. (1989). *Collaborating: Finding common ground for multiparty problems.* San Francisco: Jossey-Bass.

Gray, B., & Hay, T. (1986). Political limits to interorganizational consensus and change. *The Journal of Applied Behavioral Science, 22*(2), 95–112.

Greenfield, T. (1973). Organizations as social inventions: Rethinking assumptions about change. *Journal of Applied Behavioral Sciences, 9*(5), 551–573.

Greenleaf, R. (1977). *Servant leadership: A journey into the nature of legitimate power and greatness.* New York: Paulist Press.

Grubb, W. N., & Lazerson, M. (1982). *Broken promises: How Americans fail their children.* New York: Basic Books.

Hage, J., & Aiken, M. (1970). *Social change in complex organizations.* New York: Random House.

Hancock, R. K. (1983). The social life of the modern corporation: Changing resources and forms. In W. B. Littrell, G. Sjoberg, & L. A. Zurcher (Eds.), *Bureaucracy as a social problem* (pp. 19–36). Greenwich, CT: JAI Press.

Harbin, G., & McNulty, B. (1990). Policy implementation: Perspectives on service coordination and interagency cooperation. In S. J. Meisels & J. Shonkoff (Eds.), *Handbook of early childhood intervention* (pp. 700–721). New York: Cambridge University Press.

Harbin, G., Terry, D., & Daguio, C. (1989). *Status of the states' progress toward developing a definition for developmentally delayed as required by PL 99-457, Part H.* Chapel Hill: University of North Carolina at Chapel Hill, Carolina Institute for Child and Family Policy.

Helge, D. (1984). *Problems and strategies regarding regionalizing service delivery: Educational collaboratives in rural America.* Murray, KY: Murray State University, National Rural Research Project. (ERIC Document Reproduction Service No. ED 242 449)

Hodges, R. (1987). *Interagency cooperation: Related issues and concerns* (Council of Administrators of Special Education, Inc. information dissemination packet). Bloomington: Indiana University.

Hord, S. M. (1980, April). *Distinguishing between cooperation and collaboration: A case study approach to understanding their relative requirements and outcomes.* Paper presented at the annual meeting of the American Educational Research Association, Boston.

Hord, S. M. (1985). *Collaboration or cooperation: Comparisons and contrasts, dilemmas and decisions.* Austin: University of Texas, Research and Development Center for Teacher Education. (ERIC Document Reproduction Service No. ED 258 356)

Hord, S. M. (1986). A synthesis of research on organizational collaboration. *Educational Leadership, 43*(5), 22–26.

Houston, W. R. (1979). Collaboration—See "treason." In G. E. Hall, S. M. Hord, & G. Brown (Eds.), *Exploring issues in teacher education: Questions for future research.* Austin: The University of Texas, Research and Development Center for Teacher Education.

Hutinger, P. (Ed.). (1981, August). *Making it work in rural communities. Interagency coordination a necessity in rural programs.* Macomb: Western Illinois University Press, HCEEP Rural Network.

Infant School Society of Boston. (1828). *Constitution and by-laws.* Boston: T. R. Marvin.

Intriligator, B. A. (1986, April). *Collaboration with the schools: A strategy for school improvement*. Paper presented at the annual meeting of the American Educational Research Association, San Francisco.

Jackson, E. (1973). The present system of publicly supported day care. In D. R. Young & R. R. Nelson (Eds.), *Public policy for day care of young children* (pp. 21–46). Lexington, MA: Lexington Books.

Jacobsen, C., & Cohen, A. (1986). The power of social collectivities: Towards an integrative conceptualization and operationalization. *British Journal of Sociology, 37*(1), 106–121.

Jacobson, H. K. (1960). *American foreign policy*. New York: Random House.

Joe, T., & Nelson, D. W. (1989). New futures for America's children. In F. J. Macchiarola & A. Gartner (Eds.), *Caring for America's children* (pp. 214–223). New York: Academy of Political Science.

Johnson, H. W., McLaughlin, J. A., & Christensen, M. (1982). Interagency collaboration: Driving and restraining forces. *Exceptional Children, 48*(5), 395–399.

Jones, S. D., & Stegelin, D. A. (1988). *Ohio preschool special education interagency collaboration grant. Final report: Year one*. Unpublished manuscript. Cincinnati, OH: University of Cincinnati.

Jones, T. (1975). Some thoughts on coordination of services. *Social Work, 20*(5), 375–378.

Kagan, S. L. (1989). Early care and education: Tackling the tough issues. *Phi Delta Kappan, 70*(6), 433–439.

Kagan, S. L., Rivera, A. M., & Lamb-Parker, F. (1990). *Collaborations in action: Reshaping services for young children and their families*. New Haven, CT: Bush Center in Child Development and Social Policy.

Kahn, A. J. (1966). *Neighborhood information centers: A study and some proposals*. New York: Columbia School of Social Work.

Kahn, A. J., & Kamerman, S. B. (1987). *Child care: Facing the hard choices*. Dover, MA: Auburn House.

Kanter, R. M. (1983). *The change masters*. New York: Simon & Schuster.

Katz, A. H., & Martin, K. (1982). *A handbook of services for the handicapped*. Westport, CT: Greenwood.

Keniston, K., and the Carnegie Council on Children. (1977). *All our children: The American family under pressure*. New York: Harcourt Brace Jovanovich.

Keyserling, M. D. (1972). *Windows on day care: A report based on findings of the National Council of Jewish Women*. New York: National Council of Jewish Women.

Kraus, W. A. (1980). *Collaboration in organizations*. New York: Human Sciences Press.

Lanier, J. (1980). Collaboration session, discussant remarks. In G. E. Hall, S. M. Hord, & G. Brown (Eds.), *Exploring issues in teacher education: Questions for future research*. Austin: University of Texas, Research and Development Center for Teacher Education.

Larson, M. (1975). *Federal policy for preschool: Assumptions and evidence*. Menlo Park, CA: Stanford Research Institute.

Lazar, I., & Darlington, R. (1982). Lasting effects of early intervention: A report from the Consortium for Longitudinal Studies. *Monographs of the Society for Research in Child Development, 47*(2-3, Serial No. 195).

Lazerson, M. (1972). The historical antecedents of early childhood education. In I. J. Gordon (Ed.), *Early childhood education: The seventy-first yearbook of the National Society for the Study of Education* (pp. 33-53). Chicago, IL: University of Chicago Press.

Levine, J. (1978). *Day care and the public schools: Profiles of five communities.* Newton, MA: Education Development Center.

Levine, J. (1982). The prospects and dilemmas of child care information and referral. In E. Zigler & E. Gordon (Eds.), *Day care: Scientific and social policy options* (pp. 378-401). Boston: Auburn House.

Levy, A. (1986). Second-order planned change: Definition and conceptualization. *Organizational Dynamics, 15,* 4-20.

Levy, A., & Merry, U. (1986). *Organizational transformation: Approaches, strategies, theories.* New York: Praeger.

Levy, J. E., & Copple, C. (1989). *Joining forces: A report from the first year.* Washington, DC: National Association of State Boards of Education.

Lewin, K. (1951). *Field theory in social science.* New York: Harper & Row.

Lieberman, A. (1986). Collaborative work. *Educational Leadership, 43*(5), 4-8.

Lippitt, R., & Van Til, J. (1981). Can we achieve a collaborative community? Issues, imperatives, potentials. *Journal of Voluntary Action Research, 10*(3-4), 7-17.

Loadman, W., Parnick, Y. J., & Schober, E. (1981). *Final report evaluation/technical assistance: Community service provider.* Columbus: Ohio State University Research Foundation.

Margulies, N., & Raia, A. P. (1972). *Organizational development: Values, process, and technology.* New York: McGraw-Hill.

Martinson, M. C. (1982). Interagency services: A new era for an old idea. *Exceptional Children, 48*(5), 389-394.

Marver, J. D., & Larson, M. A. (1978). Public policy toward child care in America: A historical perspective. In P. K. Robins & S. Weiner (Eds.), *Child care and public policy* (pp. 17-42). Lexington, MA: Lexington Books.

Maryland State Department of Education (1983). Guidelines for the establishment and implementation of multiple agency approach to services. In *Perspectives on interagency collaboration.* National Invitational Symposium on Interagency Collaboration, Denver, CO. (ERIC Document Reproduction Service, No. ED 235 669)

Maximus, Inc. (1988). *An evaluability assessment of child care options for work-welfare programs* (Prepared for Assistant Secretary for Planning and Evaluation, Office of Social Services Policy, U.S. Department of Health and Human Services). Falls Church, VA: Author.

McCann, J. E. (1983). Design guidelines for social problem-solving interventions. *Journal of Applied Behavioral Science, 19,* 177-189.

McConaghy, E., & Siegel, P. (1988, November). *The challenge of child care re-*

source and referral services. Paper presented at the National Association of Child Care Resource and Referral Agencies pre-conference session of the National Association for the Education of Young Children, Anaheim, CA.

McLaughlin, M. W. (1990). The Rand Change Agent Study revisited: Macro perspectives and micro realities. *Educational Researcher, 19*(9), 11–16.

McNulty, B. (1983). Managing interagency groups. In *Perspectives on interagency collaboration*. National Invitational Symposium on Interagency Collaboration, Denver, CO. (ERIC Document Reproduction Service No. ED 235 669)

McNulty, B., & Soper, E. (1983). Critical elements of successful interagency practice. In *Perspectives on interagency collaboration*. National Invitational Symposium on Interagency Collaboration, Denver, CO. (ERIC Document Reproduction Service No. ED 235 669)

Meisels, S. J., Harbin, G., Modigliani, K., & Olson, K. (1988). Formulating optimal state early childhood intervention policies. *Exceptional Children, 55*, 159–165.

Melaville, A. I., & Blank, M. (1991). *What it takes: Structuring interagency partnerships to connect children and families with comprehensive services*. Washington, DC: Education and Human Services Consortium.

Mitchell, A. (1989). Old baggage, new visions: Shaping policy for early childhood programs. *Phi Delta Kappan, 70*(9), 664–672.

Mitchell, A., Seligson, M., & Marx, F. (1989). *Early childhood programs and the public schools*. Dover, MA: Auburn House.

Molnar, J. J. (1978). Comparative organizational properties and interorganizational interdependence. *Sociology and Social Research, 63*, 24–48.

Morgan, G. (1972). *An evaluation of the 4-C concept*. Washington, DC: Day Care and Child Development Council of America.

Morgan, G. (1989). *Asking the hard questions about child care resource and referral*. Rochester, MN: National Association of Child Care Resource and Referral Agencies.

Morgan, J. (1985, April). *Putting the pieces together: Making interagency collaboration work. Preschool interagency council: A model*. Tallahassee: Florida State Department of Education. (ERIC Document Reproduction Service No. ED 296 507)

Morris, R., & Lescohier, I. H. (1978). Service integration: Real versus illusory solutions to welfare dilemmas. In R. C. Sarri & Y. Hasenfeld (Eds.), *The management of human service* (pp. 21–50). New York: Columbia University Press.

National Academy of Sciences, National Research Council, Division of Behavioral Sciences. (1972). *Report of the Panel on the Assessment of the Community Coordinated Child Care Program*. Washington, DC: National Academy Press.

National Academy of Sciences, National Research Council, Assembly of Behavioral and Social Sciences, Committee on Child Development Research and Public Policy, Panel for the Study of the Policy Formation Process. (1982). *Making policies for children: A study of the federal process.* Washington, DC: National Academy Press.

National Academy of Sciences, National Research Council, Commission on Behavioral and Social Sciences and Education, Committee on Child Development Research and Public Policy, Panel on Child Care Policy. (1990). *Who cares for America's children? Child care policy for the 1990s.* Washington, DC: National Academy Press.

National Alliance of Business. (1989). *A blueprint for business on restructuring education.* Washington, DC: Author.

National Alliance of Business. (1990). *The Business Roundtable participation guide: A primer for business on education.* Washington, DC: Author.

National Association of State Boards of Education. (1989). *Right from the start: The report of the NASBE Task Force on Early Childhood Education.* Alexandria, VA: Author.

National Committee for the Prevention of Child Abuse. (1988, April). Newsletter. Washington, DC: Author.

National Conference of State Legislatures. (1989). *Child care and early childhood education policy: A legislator's guide.* Denver, CO: Author.

National Governors' Association. (1987). *The first sixty months: The next steps.* Washington, DC: Author.

National Governors' Association. (1990). *Educating America: State strategies for achieving the national education goals.* Washington, DC: Author.

National Institute on Drug Abuse. (1987). *National trends in drug use and related factors among American high school students and young adults.* Washington, DC: U.S. Department of Health and Human Services.

Nelson, R. R., & Young, D. R. (1973). National day care policy. In D. R. Young & R. R. Nelson (Eds.), *Public policy for day care of young children* (pp. 91–103). Lexington, MA: Lexington Books.

O'Connell, C. (1985). *How to start a school/business partnership.* Bloomington, IN: Phi Delta Kappa Educational Foundation.

O'Connor, R., Albrecht, N., Cohen, B., & Newquist-Carroll, L. (1984). *New directions in youth services: Experiences with state level coordination.* Washington, DC: U.S. Government Printing Office.

Office of Child Development. (1977). *Project Developmental Continuity: A Head Start demonstration program linking Head Start, parents and the public schools.* Washington, DC: Department of Health, Education, and Welfare, Office of Human Development.

Olsen, K. R. (1983). *Obtaining related services through local interagency collaboration.* Lexington, KY: Mid-South Regional Resource Center.

Otterbourg, S. D., & Timpane, M. (1986). Partnerships and schools. In P. Davis (Ed.), *Public-private partnerships: Improving urban life* (pp. 60–73). New York: Academy of Political Science.

Pareek, U. (1981). Developing collaboration in organizations. In *The 1981 annual handbook for group facilitators* (pp. 163–180). San Diego, CA: University Associates.

Paton, Alan. (1948). *Cry, the Beloved Country*. New York: Charles Scribner's Sons.

Paul, J. L., Stedman, D. J., & Neufeld, G. R. (Eds.). (1977). *Deinstitutionalization: Program and policy development*. Syracuse, NY: Syracuse University Press.

Pontzer, K. (1989). *Progress in state early intervention program planning under the Part H infant-toddler program: Findings of an 11-state survey*. Washington, DC: Mental Health Law Project.

Public/Private Ventures. (1990). *The practitioner's view: New challenges in serving high-risk youth*. Philadelphia, PA: Author.

Random House College Dictionary (rev. ed.). (1980). New York: Random House.

Reid, T. A., & Chandler, G. E. (1976). The evaluation of a human services network. *Journal of Community Psychology, 4*(2), 174–180.

Reid, W. (1964). Interagency co-ordination in delinquency prevention and control. *Social Service Review, 38*(4), 418–428.

Reitz, H. J. (1987). *Behavior in organizations* (3rd ed.). Homewood, IL: Irwin.

Rockefeller Brothers Foundation. (1990). *A quest for coherence in the training of early care and education teachers*. New York: Author.

Rogers, C., & Farrow, F. (1983). *Effective state strategies to promote interagency collaboration*. Washington, DC: Center for the Study of Social Policy. (ERIC Document Reproduction Service No. ED 245 467)

Rogers, D. L., & Mulford, C. L. (1982). Consequences. In D. L. Rogers, D. A. Whetten, et al. (Eds.), *Interorganizational coordination* (pp. 73–94). Ames: Iowa State University Press.

Rosewater, A. (1989). Child and family trends: Beyond the numbers. In F. J. Macchiarola & A. Gartner (Eds.), *Caring for America's children* (pp. 4–19). New York: Academy of Political Science.

Ross, E. D. (1976). *The kindergarten crusade: The establishment of preschool education in the United States*. Athens: Ohio University Press.

Scarr, S., & Weinberg, R. (1986). The early childhood enterprise: Care and education of the young. *American Psychologist, 41*(10), 1140–1146.

Schaffer, E., & Bryant, W. C. (1983). *Structures and processes for effective collaboration among local schools, colleges and universities: A collaborative project of Kannapolis City Schools*. Charlotte: Livingstone College, University of North Carolina-Charlotte. (ERIC Document Reproduction Service No. ED 225 988)

Schenet, M. A. (1982). *State education agency coordination efforts*. Washington, DC: National Institute of Education. (ERIC Document Reproduction Service No. 225 235)

Schermerhorn, J. R., Jr. (1975). Determinants of interorganizational cooperation. *Academy of Management Journal, 18*(4), 846–856.

Schindler-Rainman, E. (1981). Toward collaboration—Risks we need to take. *Journal of Voluntary Action Research, 10*(3-4), 120–127.

Schopler, J. (1987). Interorganizational groups: Origins, structures, and outcomes. *Academy of Management Review, 12*(4), 702–713.

Schorr, L. (1988). *Within our reach: Breaking the cycle of disadvantage.* New York: Anchor.

Schwartz, T. A. (1981). *An inquiry into relationships between human services agencies: Danville (VA)* (Research Report 81-107). Charlottesville: University of Virginia. (ERIC Document Reproduction Service No. ED 215 196)

Siegel, P. (1983). Child care information and referral services: Where are we in 1983? *Child Care Information and Referral National Quarterly, 1*(1), pp. 2–4.

Skaff, L. F. (1988). Child maltreatment coordinating committees for effective service delivery. *Child Welfare, 67*(3), 217–230.

Skerry, P. (1978). *Mediating structures and child care policy* (unpublished draft for the Mediating Structures Project). Washington, DC: American Enterprise Institute.

Skinner, S. J., & Guiltinan, J. P. (1986). Extra-network linkages, dependence and power. *Social Forces, 64*(3), 702–713.

Slater, P. (1970). *The pursuit of loneliness: American culture at the breaking point.* Boston: Beacon.

Smith, K., & Berg, D. (1987). *Paradoxes of group life.* San Francisco: Jossey-Bass.

Stafford, B. G., Rog, D., & Vander Meer, P. (1984, June). *A review of literature on coordination, an annotated bibliography and a survey of other collaborative efforts.* Nashville: Tennessee Children's Services Commission. (ERIC Document Reproduction Service No. ED 251 235)

Steiner, G. Y. (1976). *The children's cause.* Washington, DC: Brookings Institution.

Steinfels, M. (1973). *Who's minding the children? The history and politics of day care in America.* New York: Simon & Schuster.

Sugarman, J. (1989). Federal support revisited. In F. J. Macchiarola & A. Gartner (Eds.), *Caring for America's children* (pp. 99–109). New York: Academy of Political Science.

Tank, R. M. (1980). *Young children, families and society in America since the 1820s: The evolution of health, education and child care programs for preschool children.* Doctoral dissertation, Department of History, University of Michigan, Ann Arbor. (University Microfilms No. 8106233)

Tindall, L. W., Gugerty, J., Getzel, E. E., Salin, J., Wacker, G. B., & Crowley, C. B. (1982, January). *Handbook on developing effective linking strategies: Vocational models for linking agencies serving the handicapped.* Madison: University of Wisconsin (ERIC Document Reproduction Service No. ED 215 097)

Tocqueville, A. de. (1947). *Democracy in America* (H. Reeve, Trans.). New York: Oxford University Press. (Original work published 1838)

Trist, E. (1976). Toward a postindustrial culture. In M. Dunnetter (Ed.), *Hand-*

book of industrial and organizational psychology (pp. 1011–1033). Chicago: Rand McNally.

Trist, E. (1977). Collaboration in work settings: A personal perspective. *The Journal of Applied Behavioral Science, 13*(3), 268–278.

Trist, E. (1983). Referent organizations and the development of inter-organizational domains. *Human Relations, 36*(3), 269–284.

Trohanis, P. (1989). *A brief introduction to P.L. 99-457.* Chapel Hill: University of North Carolina at Chapel Hill, Frank Porter Graham Child Development Center.

Turquet, P. M. (1974). Leadership: The individual and the group. In G. S. Gibbard, J. J. Hartman, & R. D. Mann (Eds.), *Analysis of groups* (pp. 349–371). San Francisco: Jossey-Bass.

U.S. budget in brief: Fiscal year 1990. (1989). Washington, DC: U.S. Government Printing Office.

U.S. Bureau of Justice Statistics. (1986). *Preventing domestic violence against women* (Special Report). Washington, DC: Author.

U.S. Department of Education. (1986). *Thesaurus of ERIC descriptors* (10th ed.). Phoenix, AZ: Oryx Press.

U.S. Department of Labor. (1988). *Child care: A workforce issue* (Report of the Secretary's Task Force). Washington, DC: Author.

U.S. House of Representatives. (1972, October 11). *Comprehensive Child Development Act, Report with minority and additional views* (No. 92-1570). Washington, DC.

Urban and Rural Systems Associates. (1977). *Provider services network project* (Draft Final Report). San Jose, CA: Santa Clara County Office of Education. (ED 148 484).

Van de Ven, A. H. (1976). On the nature, formation, and maintenance of relations among organizations. *Academy of Management Review, 1*(4), 24–36.

Warren, R. L. (1973). Comprehensive planning and coordination: Some functional aspects. *Social Problems, 20*(3), 355–364.

Webster's Third International Dictionary. (1981). Springfield, MA: Merriam-Webster.

Weiss, J. A. (1981). Substance vs. symbol in administrative reform: The case of human services coordination. *Policy Analysis, 7*, 21–46.

Whitebook, M., Howes, C., & Phillips, D. (1989). *Who cares? Child care teachers and the quality of care in America* (Executive Summary, National Child Care Staffing Study). Oakland, CA: Child Care Employee Project.

Wilson, W. J. (1987). *The truly disadvantaged: The inner city, the underclass, and public policy.* Chicago: University of Chicago Press.

Woolsey, S. H. (1977). Pied Piper politics and the child-care debate. *Daedalus, 106*(2), 127–145.

Wu, P. C. (1986, November). *Research on collaboration: Why it works in some places and not in others.* Paper presented at the annual meeting of the National Council of States on Inservice Education, Lexington, KY.

Yin, R. K. (1989). *Case study research: Design and methods.* Newbury Park, CA: Sage.

Zeller, R. W. (1980). Direction service: Collaboration one case at a time. In J. O. Elder & P. R. Magrab (Eds.), *Coordinating services to handicapped children* (pp. 65–97). Baltimore: Brookes.

Zigler, E., & Hunsinger, S. (1977). Bringing up day care. *APA Monitor, 8*(43), 8–9.

Index

About the Author

SHARON LYNN KAGAN is the Senior Associate of the Bush Center in Child Development and Social Policy at Yale University. Combining scholarly work in academia and practical work in the fields of early care and education, parent involvement and family support, and organizational change, Dr. Kagan's research and policy work is recognized nationally and internationally. She is a frequent consultant to the White House, Congress, the U.S. Departments of Education and Health and Human Services, and numerous national foundations and associations. A Governing Board Member of the National Association for the Education of Young Children and the Family Resource Coalition, among others, Dr. Kagan participates on numerous national research and policy panels, including the Chapter I National Evaluation Panel, the National Head Start Evaluation Design Panel, the White House–National Governors' Association Education Goals Readiness Resource Panel, the Head Start Silver Anniversary Panel, and the National Association of State Boards of Education Early Childhood Panels.

Author of more than 60 articles and editor of the National Society for the Study of Education Ninetieth Yearbook, *Early Care and Education: Obstacles and Opportunities*, Dr. Kagan has co-edited three books—*Children, Families and Government* (Cambridge University Press, 1983); *America's Family Support Programs* (Yale University Press, 1987); and *Early Schooling: The National Debate* (Yale University Press, 1988)—and special issues of *Phi Delta Kappan* on early care and education and the *Early Childhood Research Quarterly* on educating culturally and linguistically diverse preschoolers. In addition, her research and writing have focused on improving schools and other institutions that serve young children and families, the role of schools in the delivery of human services, the role of parents in their children's development, similarities and differences in profit and nonprofit child care, and strategies for collaboration among the institutions that serve young children.

Dr. Kagan's research and policy work is augmented by practical experience at the local, state, and federal level. She has worked in Head Start, the public schools, a state department of education, the U.S. Senate and, while on leave from Yale, as director of the Mayor's Office of Early Childhood Education in New York City.